S0-ECN-903

SMOKING BEHAVIOUR FROM PRE-ADOLESCENCE TO YOUNG ADULTHOOD

Smoking Behaviour from Pre-Adolescence to Young Adulthood

ANTHONY VICTOR SWAN
MICHAEL MURRAY
LINDA JARRETT

United Medical and Dental Schools
St Thomas's Hospital

HV
5745
. S93
1991
west

Avebury

Aldershot · Brookfield USA · Hong Kong · Singapore · Sydney

© A. V. Swan, M. Murray and L. Jarrett 1991

All rights reserved. No part of this publication may be reproduced, stored in a retrieval system, or transmitted in any form or by any means, electronic, mechanical, photocopying, recording, or otherwise without the prior permission of Gower Publishing Company Limited.

Published by
Avebury
Gower Publishing Company Limited
Gower House
Croft Road
Aldershot
Hants GU11   3HR
England

Gower Publishing Company
Old Post Road
Brookfield
Vermont 05036
USA

ISBN 1 85628 033 0

Printed in Great Britain by
Billing & Sons Ltd, Worcester

Contents

List of tables

List of figures

Acknowledgements

This study owes most to the children and their parents in Derbyshire, who made the effort to complete the questionnaires. The organisation and analysis over the years was an immense task and was only posible with the strenous and ingenious efforts of many individuals. Contributions ranged from questionnaire design, administration, complex computing to statistical analysis, interpretation and presentation. The personnel, in order of appearance were: Professor W W Holland, Dr B Bewley, Dr A V Swan, I Day, V Polland, J M Bland, M Banks, M Johnson, D V Clyde, M Murray, A Cracknell, G Enock, S Kiryluk, G Clarke, L Jarrett, R Ruman, R Creeser and R Maric.

Financial support was provided by the MRC through a number of grants and by the Department of Health through research unit staff.

This particular text owes much to the secretarial efforts of Yvonne Smith. However, the quality of the final 'typeset' appearance is almost entirely due to the skilful efforts of Sundhiya Mandalia with our desk top publishing facilities.

Summary

In the early 1970 there was considerable concern at the magnitude of the public health problem due to adult smoking and the lack of success in school anti-smoking campaigns. Prompted by this the MRC funded an investigation of the development of smoking behaviour in Derbyshire secondary school children. This text presents the design, analysis and results of that study obtained from following over 6000 children through adolescence to young adulthood.

In 1974 about 6300 children entered the study, in the first year of secondary school when they were 11-12 years old, and were followed through to the fifth year when they were 15-16 years old. During that time data was obtained each year on their own and their families' smoking behaviour, their attitudes and their social activities. At the beginning and end of the school period information was also obtained from the children's parents on their attitudes and smoking behaviour. In 1981 the children were followed-up with a brief postal questionnaire to which 5610 (71.2%) responded and finally a comprehensive follow-up postal survey was carried out in 1984 to which 4737 (60.2%) responded.

The analyses presented here are concerned with:

(i) identifying and quantifying the associations between the childrens early characteristics and later smoking using logistic regression analyses;

(ii) assessing how the rates of uptake of smoking vary with age and other factors using lifetable techniques to obtain and compare uptake curves;

and

(iii) comparing the chronology of changes in smoking behaviour and changes in attitude to investigate whether they are consistent with causal relationships between attitudes and behaviour that might be influenced by health education.

The main findings are that:

(i) 30% of smoking in young adulthood can be attributed to the child's attitudes to peer pressure and the hazards of smoking as they are at 11-12 years and exposure to parental smoking;

(ii) more than 70% will try smoking before the age of sixteen irrespective of their attitudes and circumstances, but only about 3.5% will try subsequently;

(iii) about 45% will try regular smoking by 16 years dependent on attitudes and family environment, but only about 4.6% will do so subsequently;

(iv) there is a clear maximum incidence of about 20% as children move into the third year of secondary school;

(v) there is a clear pattern of attitudes becoming more tolerant to smoking before the children take up regular smoking;

The text concludes with a discussion of how health education programmes could take account of the findings and the magnitude of effects that might be achieved by such programmes.

1 Introduction

Smoking in adults is generally accepted to be the cause of long and short term health problems. Although some of the penalties are immense the risks are not obviously high for the individual and between 30 and 40% of the adult population smoke regularly (OPCS: 1984 General Household Survey 1982). This high prevalence combined with even small risks of lung cancer, increased heart disease and all the chronic respiratory problems associated with smoking are sufficient to generate a large public health problem and generates a large cost to the Health Service. However, depending on social policy this does not necessarily mean a large overall cost to the community when pension implications are taken into account (Leu and Schaub;1983). Nonetheless, it is clearly necessary to address the public health problem and for the community to ensure that individuals are not unwitting victims of influences they may not detect and cannot evade.

For adults the arguments may not be totally convincing that they should be stopped, harassed or in other ways protected from a drug habit that is generally less harmful to themselves and others than even alcohol let alone cocaine and 'harder' drugs. However, in many cases this is behaviour learned during childhood or adolescence and the adult when sufficiently informed of the consequences, may not be able to make a free choice in the face of pharmacological and/or psychological addiction acquired during that period. It seems highly appropriate that children should be at least guided away from acquiring harmful and anti social habits until they have reached an age of discretion. It appears that individuals not smoking before the age of 16 years rarely take it up subsequently so one may assume that after that age discretion dictates abstinence. Since there are no obvious benefits to acquiring the habit at any age it seems appropriate to ensure that the decision on whether or not to smoke is delayed until after that age for as many individuals as possible.

On the assumption that this is the appropriate point of view for society to take, it is necessary to consider how best to deter children from smoking prior to reaching the age of sixteen.

Many Health Education and anti-smoking programmes have been tried in the UK and elsewhere (Thompson; 1978). They have generally managed to detect a change in knowledge of the health risks, but the effect on the prevalence and incidence of smoking has rarely been detectable let alone of practical importance. It was in the light of this lack of success in health education that the Medical Research Council encouraged and financed the study reported here in an attempt to obtain new insight into the factors involved in the evolution of smoking behaviour in children.

The study was designed to follow a cohort of 11 year olds through five years of secondary school. The intention was to observe how, over this period of their lives, their smoking behaviour changed and how this was related to their attitudes, the nature of their family, social and school environment and to their health. The precise design of the study is discussed in greater detail below. The particular aim of this text is to assess quantitatively what we have learned from this cohort on the way in which children start or do not start smoking and the consequent health effects in order to estimate what may be achieved by better health education programs. The study has generated a considerable amount of unique descriptive information on children's behaviour, health and attitudes which is of interest in itself, but the primary concern of the text is to illustrate the methodology necessary to make the best use of such data and to deduce what has been learned of use for future health education programs and to estimate what may and may not be achieved by health education in terms of reducing child and adult smoking.

2 Review of the literature

Historical Background

From 1905 to 1945 the consumption of cigarettes per head per annum rose steadily in both sexes although it was much lower in women, 750 to 4,500 in men and 0 to 1250 in women Figure 1 (Lee 1976).

There was a marked drop after the 1939-45 war, but consumption began to rise again in both sexes until the first Royal College of Physicians report entitled 'Smoking and Health' in 1962. (RCP 1962). Subsequently consumption in men fell again and although it fluctuated, with another drop after the 1971 RCP report quickly reversed by an equivalent increase, there did not seem to be a trend in either direction until after 1975. Among women, on the other hand, consumption increased steadily throughout this period almost irrespective of the RCP reports. After 1975 there was a steadily decline in the consumption of both men and women.

Consumption of manufactured cigarettes in the U.K

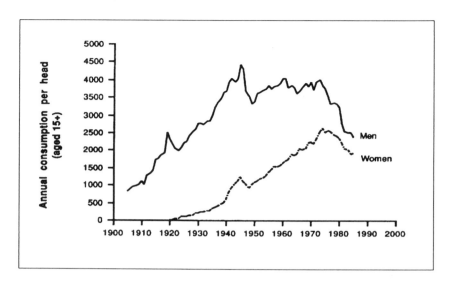

During this time the evidence for serious health consequences from smoking steadily mounted. A landmark was the research by Hammond and Horn (1958) which reported a follow-up study over nearly four years of 187,783 men between the ages of 50 and 69. This study showed that mortality from cancer was higher in cigarette smokers and pipe and cigar smokers than in men who had never smoked and the mortality ratio of cigarette smokers to non-smokers increased with the number of cigarettes smoked per day. Deaths from all causes were considerably higher among smokers than among non-smokers (SMR = 1.57) with coronary heart disease accounting for 52.1% of the excess and cancer for 26.0% (lung cancer 13.5%). The study also showed that the higher rates in smokers rapidly decreased once they ceased smoking. Sir Richard Doll (1984) reviewing Hammond and Horn's work 26 years later concluded that the findings had been broadly true and had had a profound influence on policies for preventive medicine.

Doll and Hill (1964) followed a cohort of doctors over much the same period and observed that while cigarette consumption changed little in the general population and lung cancer mortality increased 7%, among the doctors 50% of the smokers ceased smoking and mortality from lung cancer in doctors fell by 38%.

The Royal College of Physicians report (RCP; 1962) was aimed at bringing this evidence to the attention of the general public in an attempt to stem the rising mortality and morbidity due to what had long been seen as a relatively harmless and pleasurable habit.

Smoking in Children

Concern for adults suffering unexpected consequences from their smoking behaviour led naturally to a concern for the adults of tomorrow who as schoolchildren had been learning that smoking was a popular and pleasurable adult activity. From 1959 onwards there was a number of cross sectional studies investigating the prevalence of smoking among children of all ages from 10 years upwards. As prevalence estimates from small studies are not very reliable, this review is restricted to those with sample sizes over 3000. Chave et al (1959) in a study of 3,479 children discovered that nearly 10% of 12-13 year old boys were regularly smoking five or more cigarettes a week. Among the 15-16 year olds these authors found the prevalence of such smoking to be 27.6%. The figures for girls were much lower ranging from 0.4% up to 4.9%. Subsequent authors felt that at these ages that one cigarette a week consistently was evidence of a regular habit and most studies from then on reported their findings in terms of the prevalence of children regularly smoking more than one per week. Bothwell (1959) found 18.5% of boys and 3.9% of girls regularly smoking more than one per week at 12-13 years of age with 38.6% and 15.6% among the 15-16 year olds. In 1965 Holland and Elliot studying over 9000 children found prevalences of 19.1% and 3.9% in the 12-13 years old boys and girls and 26.1% and 17.1% in the 15-16 years olds. In 1970 O'Rourke found in over 5000 Dublin secondary school children equivalent prevalences at 12-13 years and 15-16 years of 24.9% and 37.8% among the boys and 2.8%, 24.6% among the girls. There was clearly a large proportion of children acquiring some sort of smoking habit. Admittedly the rate of uptake with age could not be established from this cross-sectional data. In addition because the studies ranged over different types of school, urban and rural locations and two countries, England and Ireland, it was not possible to identify unambiguously, any general tendency for the smoking among 11 year olds (say) to increase or decrease over time. Nonetheless it was clear that the problem was common, widespread and not diminishing.

The Impact of Health Education

As these findings emerged it became obvious to health educationists that it was necessary to alert the children to the dangers and consequences of smoking in an attempt to deter them. As a result, many anti-smoking campaigns were mounted in different parts of the country. Although they were not generally organised for evaluation by proper research methods a number of studies in schools with and without such campaigns produced findings by which their impact could be judged. Bynner (Bynner, JM; 1969) studied children from 60 schools and although he found evidence that the campaigns increased awareness of the risks of smoking he found little evidence that they reduced the prevalence of smoking. Two studies, by Watson (Watson, LM; 1966) and Jefferys et al (1967) set out to evaluate specific types of anti-smoking campaign. Watson's study was a very carefully designed investigation of four different health education methods applied to nearly 800 children. These methods extended from - an intensive didactic approach using lectures, films, debates and a health quiz; through - group discussions with trained group leaders and psychological persuasion using oblique techniques such as 'debunking advertising' in group meetings; to - a 'total project' approach where all the above approaches were used in combination and the children's parents were also involved through letters and invitations to meetings.

There was evidence over a period of four months, for a reduction in smoking particularly in the didactic group where the reduction was significant in the boys from 33% to 21.6%. However, in this study a child was defined as a smoker by any answer to 'how many cigarettes do you smoke weekly?' other than none. This included no answer at all. For this reason and the possibility of biased responses it is difficult to justify treating these findings as strong evidence of health education genuinely reducing smoking even in the short term. Jefferys' study showed that an anti-smoking campaign directed at 13 year olds had no effect on the prevalence of smoking either at the time or five years later. At the end of the 1960's the evidence suggested a need for deeper and more precise knowledge of the social and psychological processes involved in the uptake of smoking in children. It was felt that with more knowledge of the sequence of changes in behaviour and attitudes it would be possible to determine the optimum content, form and timing of health education programmes and their likely impact. this led to the design and funding of the study reported here.

Subsequent findings in Childrens Smoking During the ten year course of the study there have been a number of cross-sectional studies. The most comprehensive of these was by Dobbs and Marsh (1983). In England and Wales, from sample of just under 3000, they found that the prevalence of children regularly smoking one or more cigarettes a week ranged, for the boys, from 1% in the first year of secondary school to 26% in the fifth year. In girls the equivalent figures were 0% to 29%. It appears that there has been a decline in smoking among boys. Compared with the findings in the late 1960's the boys prevalences found by Marsh and Dobbs in 1983 are markedly lower throughout this school period.

Their figures for the girls however, although lower in the early years are much the same as the boys by the fifth year and thus nearly twice the prevalence figures found for girls at this age (15-16 years) in the late 1960's. It appears that the same pattern as has been seen in adult smoking is being echoed among the children. The boys prevalences appear to have reached a peak sometime in the 1970's and started to decline while the girls prevalences appear to be still rising. Even so more than one in four children in their fifth year of secondary school are regularly smoking one or more cigarettes a week and it remains a sizeable problem. Reid (1985) commenting on the Dobbs and Marsh results observes that they support previous findings to the effect that health education needs to be given before the children reach 13 years of age. He also observes, referring to a report by Wilcox and Gillies (1982) that most health education concerned with smoking is deferred until the children are between 14 and 16 years old. This does not appear to have been much discussed in the earlier literature although all the prevalence studies show the greatest differences between the ages of 12 and 14 years. These studies do not give incidence estimates, but the difference in prevalence between two years can be taken as such on the assumption that any change from year to year is the same in both age groups. On this assumption the incidence appears, from the majority of studies, to be greatest between 12.5 and 14.5 years in both sexes. Obviously a longitudinal study could confirm this unambiguously.

The Efficacy of Anti-smoking Health Education

During the period of the study there was a considerable amount of activity, particularly in the US, concerned with implementing, and in some cases evaluating, school based anti-smoking programmes.

However in the early years as Thompson pointed out in his review (1978) "most methods have shown little success". In 1979 the US Surgeon General observed that 'most of the programmes are not based on any sound theoretical model, but rather on what people think might work - or what seems reasonable to them at the time." (US Surgeon General; 1979).

It was not surprising that the success of these programmes was rather limited.

One exception however was the school health Curriculum project initially developed in Berkely, California and evaluated by Milne and co-workers (Milne, A et al; 1975) who reported some modest successes. In the mid seventies the Health Education Council in conjunction with the City of Sheffield Education Department developed a modification of this project for use in British Schools. This revised version known as the HEC 'My Body' project is fully described by Wilcox and co-workers (1978). The project was implemented in the last year of a number of Sheffield primary schools when the children were 10-11 years old. Murray, Swan et al (1982) reported an evaluation of this project. The results indicated slight evidence of a lowered prevalence of smoking at 11-12 years in the boys, but not in girls. However, the prevalence at that age is very low and changes are difficult to detect. There was much stronger evidence of an increase in the children's knowledge of the hazards of smoking and of beneficial effects on their attitudes to smoking.

Over the same period there have been a sequence of studies reviewed by Reid (1985) which have, at least in the short term, achieved some success in reducing smoking as well as changing attitudes and increasing knowledge. Reid's review is primarily concerned to identify the effective factors in health education programmes. He quotes Perry et al (1983) and Arkin et al (1981) as finding little difference between health education programmes concerned with long term health risks and those concerned with social pressures. The conclusion is that 'scare tactics' should not be abandoned too readily. However, Reid reports that during the 1970's the trend was towards programmes based on increasing self-esteem referred to as 'person-centred' approaches. These approaches, Reid observes, need to take into account the influence of peers, siblings and parents. This includes not only their behaviour, but also their attitudes as the child perceives them. For example McGuffin (1982) found that 58% of 15-16 year olds who had tried smoking and then given up cited parental disapproval as a factor. Nelson et al (1985) reported that "....teenager's reports of their parent's attitudes .... was more predictive of whether they smoked than was their parent's smoking status." Clearly there is a need for information on the magnitude of these effects and how much health education programs aimed at influencing or counteracting them can be expected to achieve if future health education programmes are to be designed effectively.

The cohort study described in this text was mounted with the intention of providing that information and it is clear that the need still exists. The longitudinal data now available from this study provides a unique opportunity for assessing the form, degree and chronology involved in the associations between factors influencing the children's smoking behaviour and how that behaviour develops right through adolescence to young adulthood.

3 Methods

3.1 Study Design

The design of any study is largely implicit in the precise specification of the research questions to be answered. The questions determine the general structure of the study design required, the broad data requirements and the main analyses.

In this case the questions arose from a belief that effective health education required more precise knowledge of the circumstances, attitudes and behaviour of children acquiring the habit early, late or not at all. The questions were: what factors determine if and when children take up smoking? how might these be used in a health education programme? what might be achieved if they were? and finally what are the immediate health consequences of adolescent smoking? To answer these would, ideally, require the regular observation of one or more cohorts of children from an age when none were smoking until all who were to become smokers had done so, that is from about 7 to 25 years of age. Such a lengthy and potentially large research project was unlikely to be the most effective use of research resources so it was considered necessary to restrict the study in a number of ways. Firstly it was decided that there was no need for more than one cohort. Secondly, evidence suggested that the majority (3/4) of the 40% adult smokers had acquired the habit by the age of 16 years

(Bynner;1966). It was also clear that tracing the 60% or more of children who leave secondary school at 16 (London Borough of Merton; 1986) would be costly. The study was therefore limited to one of following children up to the 5th year of secondary school when they would be between the ages of 15 to 16 years. At the other end of the age range it was clear that the administrative problems of collecting data from children in a number of primary schools up to their 11th Year and then keeping track of them as a cohort as they were dispersed through the secondary school system would be immense and a study of health education in Sheffield (Murray et al; 1982) confirmed that this would have been the case.

A pilot study in over 8000 final year Derbyshire primary school children aged 10-11.5 years showed that the prevalence of regular smoking (one or more per week) was 6.9% in boys and 2.6% in girls. (Bewley, Halil and Snaith; 1973). Thus although these were worrying figures they showed that the bulk of children starting to smoke at school would not do so until their secondary school period. In addition to this it was clear that keeping track of a complete cohort, initially identified in primary schools as they went in many different directions to their respective secondary schools would present a daunting administrative problem. Accordingly the study was designed to follow a cohort of children during their first five years in secondary school.

The objectives of the study were:

1. To describe the change in prevalence of smoking in children from age 11 to 16 years;
2. To describe how attitudes, behaviour, circumstances and environment were associated with the development of smoking during this period;
and
3. To assess what factors might be of use in identifying more efficient health education programmes and to estimate the effect that might be achieved.

Implicit in these broad objectives was the intention to obtain a number of precise estimates. These included the incidence of smoking at each age in various subgroups of children and other quantitative aspects of their developing smoking behaviour. It was also clear that the analysis would involve testing various hypotheses concerning associations between risk factors and the uptake of smoking. These were used to estimate the lower limits of the sample size required.

It was estimated that prevalences of regular smoking (>1/week) by the age of 15-16 years would be at least 20%. The aim was to detect as significant the effect of characteristics of the child's environment e.g. mothers smoking, which increased a prevalence of this magnitude by a factor of about 1.3. That is, the study needed to be large enough to detect as significant relative risks associated with such influences as mothers smoking compared to neither parent smoking, of 1.3 or more. This in turn meant that the sample size needed to be large enough to show the difference between 0.2 and 0.26 as significant at the 5% level and to have the power to ensure that if the population 'true' difference was of this magnitude then there was an 80% chance that the observed differences would reach significance. Using the method described in Casagrande et al (1978) it can be calculated that the sample size required is 804 in each group or 1608 in total. If we anticipate that boys and girls may differ and need to be tested separately and that of the four categories: Neither parent smoking, mother only, father only and both parents the first two will contain about half the children than we need $1608 + 1608 = 3216$ boys and the same number of girls i.e. 6432 in total.

Fortunately, interest in the Derbyshire health and education department meant that there was no difficulty in obtaining the cooperation of as many schools as required. In addition to this, because that department was willing to handle a large quantity of data processing on their own computer, the sample size did not have to be much restricted for administrative reasons.

Accordingly it was decided to aim for a sample of about 8000 children in the expectation that non-response due to out of date class lists and so on would still leave a large enough sample for estimates to be sufficiently precise and tests of hypotheses to have more than adequate power.

The final design included 48 schools where the headteacher agreed to participate in providing the main cohort of children and two substudies involving a further 10 schools. It was decided that the main cohort, identified by X's in (Figure 2) should be the 11-12 year olds entering these 48 secondary schools in 1974. The data were to be collected from the children once a year until their fifth year in 1978. It was also decided to collect data from the children's parents using a postal questionnaire in the first and fifth years. Finally, information was also obtained directly from the teachers and head teachers in the 48 schools.

The two substudies were concerned with assessing the levels of certain biases which potentially may affect the results of long cohort studies. Firstly, to assess whether the process of studying the children in this way affected their smoking behaviour, the so-called Hawthorne effect (Roethlisberger and Dickson; 1939), a further four schools were identified for a survey only in the fifth year 1978 (H in Figure 2). Secondly, to assess what secular trends were occurring during the study period six further schools were included so that 11-

12 year olds in 1977, when the cohort reached 14-15 years, could be compared with the cohort when they were 11-12 years old in 1974. A group of 14-15 year olds in these schools were also surveyed in 1974 to compare with the cohort when they reached that age in 1977. These are identified as S in Figure 2. This constituted the entire study design as proposed to and funded by the MRC in 1973.

However, it was subsequently decided that it would be useful to follow the main cohort into adulthood and in 1981 the MRC funded an extension to the study. This involved a sequence of three studies a pilot and then a two stage full follow-up. The pilot consisted of a brief postal questionnaire in 1981, when the cohort was 18-19 years old, to assess the likely response rate for a full follow-up postal survey. That having proved successful the full follow up study was started with an in depth interview of a small sample in 1982 to generate hypotheses on which to base a questionnaire on adult smoking in various environments (I in Figure 2). Finally in 1984 when the cohort was 21-22 years old the follow-up questionnaire was sent by post to all members of the cohort for whom addresses were available.

Figure 2:

Study design

Age	74	75	76	77	78	79	80	81	82	83	84
Prospective group											
11-12yrs	X			S							
12-13		X									
13-14			X								
14-15	S			X							
15-16					X						
16-17											
17-18											
18-19							X				
19-20								I			
20-21											
21-22											X
Control group						H					
Parents		P				P					
Teachers		T	T			T					

14

3.2 The Sample

The sampling frame available was largely determined by administrative circumstances. It was only feasible to mount such a large study in close co-operation with the local health and education department. Since we had close links with Derbyshire there were very good practical reasons why the study should take place there. It is possible that there are systematic differences in prevalence between different parts of the country although there is no strong evidence of this. This might mean that estimates of prevalence from the study might not be applicable to children in other areas and that possibility has to be considered in the analysis.

However, the important analyses in this investigation are comparisons of subgroups within the sample to assess the associations between characteristics of the children and their environment and their uptake of smoking. This means that results will only be biassed because the sample is unrepresentative if it is more so in some subgroups than it is in others. For example the Derbyshire children may smoke less than those in London, but as long as this affects boys and girls equally estimates of the difference between the sexes will be unaffected. Nonetheless the possibility that there are differential biases must always be borne in mind and the problem is discussed further when we consider the effects of non-response.

3.3 Data

The data collected from each source at each stage are comprehensively specified by the questionnaires in Appendix I. The questionnaires to the main cohort children enquired closely into their smoking and social activities and into their attitudes to a variety of matters including smoking and hazards associated with smoking. These data were collected, sometimes with minor modifications, for each year throughout the school period 1974-78. The parents' questionnaire at the beginning and end of the school period elicited information on the child's health, on their own smoking and their attitudes to various aspects of education and smoking.

The teachers' and headteachers' questionnaires were used to obtain data on the teachers attitudes and smoking behaviour and on the school regulations and environment generally. The Hawthorne and secular trend sub-studies were restricted to children and only included questions on smoking behaviour and basic demographic characteristics. The 1981 pilot follow-up was a very brief postal questionnaire on smoking habits, occupation, marital status and health.

The interview study produced a range of data from complete transcripts of lengthy semi-structured, but free ranging, interviews. The full postal follow-up questionnaire included a very comprehensive enquiry into the structure of their work environment as well as their smoking habits, social activities and their health attitudes and practices.

3.4 Analysis

The data set provides information on the children, their attitudes, behaviour and environment for each age range at which they are surveyed. At the simplest level the study can be considered as a sequence of cross-sectional surveys each of which provides descriptive information on the proportions of children in various categories who smoke, behave in particular ways or hold particular attitudes. In addition regression models, linear on the logistic scale (Dyke and Patterson; 1952, The GLIM manual; 1985) can be fitted to assess the form and magnitude of associations between various characteristics of the children and their environment and their smoking behaviour, health and attitudes. During the period of the study a number of papers reporting this type of cross-sectional analysis have been published (Appendix III).

The longitudinal nature of the data considerably extends the range of analytical possibilities. Analyses of smoking, health, attitudes and other behaviour at the later ages comparing children categorised according to earlier personal and environmental characteristics are possible. Relationships between later behaviour and earlier characteristics can be investigated by fitting logistic regression models to estimate how much the earlier characteristics can be used to predict later behaviour. Such models indicate what temporal relation-ships exist that may be causal and could be used to benefit health education programmes. In addition the time of discrete changes in smoking behaviour during the period can be described and modelled with methods such as those of Cox (1972) for survival curves. This allows the pattern of uptake as the children get older to be compared for various categories of children and may cast light on the optimum timing of health education designed to influence the development of behaviour and attitudes. Finally the patterns of change in behaviour and attitudes within children can be summarised and described and insofar as clear groups are identified the health education implications for such grouping can be assessed and the factors useful in predicting to which grouping given children belong can be identified.

The results of the study and these analyses allow the magnitude of the health and smoking problem to be estimated at each stage as the children develop through secondary school and into young adulthood. The factors associated with the development of smoking behaviour and health problems can be identified, the magnitude of their effects can be estimated and their relative importance assessed. The way in which health problems, smoking behaviour and attitudes develop can be accurately described. Finally the possible effects of health education programmes on smoking and health can be estimated. In particular it will be possible to estimate the effects of deterring children from experimenting with smoking before particular stages in their school career.

3.5 Bias Due to Differential Non-response

Children who smoke appear more likely to drop outs of the study. This means that over time the prevalences of smoking observed in each year considered as cross-sectional surveys will be biassed downwards from that in the general population of such children. In the subsamples of children with complete sequences of data this bias is likely to become quite severe and thus they are not appropriate for obtaining prevalence estimates. Fortunately comparisons internal to the data set are not necessarily biassed at all and can be interpreted relatively safely with a few minor assumptions. This can be illustrated by using parental smoking as reported by the children and assessing how a higher non-response among the smoking children affects estimates of how the prevalence differs from one parental smoking category to another. Table 1 gives the observed prevalences of smoking in 15-16 year old boys (1978) by parental smoking groups.

Table 1:

Effects of differential non-response on prevalence estimates
(Boys aged 15-16 years)

Parental Smoking	N	Observed Prevalences	Estimated Prevalences	
			If smokers respond less[1]	If non-smokers affected by parents and own smoking[2]
Neither	670	0.13	0.14	0.14
Mother	293	0.22	0.23	0.24
Father	480	0.20	0.21	0.22
Both	580	0.27	0.28	0.31
Total	2032	0.20	0.21	0.22

[1] *Non-response is assumed here to be 5% in non-smokers, 10% in Smokers*
[2] *Non-response is here assumed to be an extra 5% for non-smokers and 10% or smokers for each smoking parent. it is thus 5%, 10%, 10% and 15% or non-smokers and 10%, 20%, 20% and 30% for the smokers in the or categories.*

The second column shows what the true prevalences consistent with the observed would be if the response rates were 95% in non-smokers and 90% in smokers. The bias in the observed prevalences is quite small for this pattern of non response e.g. the prevalence among children when neither parent smokes of 14% is observed as 13%. There is even less effect on comparisons of the children in different parental smoking categories. For example the effect of mother only smoking which is 23% - 14% = 9% is observed as 22%-13% = 9%. There is also the possibility the response rates may differ according to parental smoking which would affect comparisons of the parental smoking groups.

However, as can be seen from column 3 which gives the true prevalences consistent with those observed on the assumption that each smoking parent decreases the response rate of smoking children by 10% and that of the non-smoking children by 5%. Again the effects are relatively small although they do show that estimates of the effect of parental smoking will be biassed in these circumstances. For example the effect of both parents smoking which is 31% - 22% = 9% is observed as 27%-20% = 7%. This illustrates that factors positively associated with an increase in smoking which increase non-response most in smokers will cause biases which diminish their apparent effects. Thus the effects of such factors will be under rather than over-estimated. However, the difference between the smoking and non-smoking response rates is not much affected by other factors and in most of the analyses it will be assumed not to matter although the possibility will be taken into account when appropriate.

3.6 Statistical Techniques - Logistic Regression

To investigate the associations of various factors with the prevalence of early smoking it was necessary to fit linear models. By this means the variations in prevalence associated with various risk factors acting separately and together can be assessed and estimated as 'effects' in the statistical sense. The analysis is required to summarise how groups of children with different combinations of risk factors differ in their smoking prevalence. For each group of children there is a number at risk and a number classified as smokers. The number smoking is a binomial variable and hence the way it varies from one group to another is not appropriately summarised by models fitted by the standard least squares regression method. It is necessary to use what are known as Maximum likelihood methods and fit so-called logistic regression models (Dyke and Patterson; 1952).

Logistic regression analysis produces a set of regression coefficients closely equivalent to those obtained with least squares multi-linear regression. The main difference relevant to their interpretation is that the coefficients from logistic regression represent average distances on the log (odds) scale. Note that the odds of a child being a smoker in a particular group of n children is the ratio of the number that are *(r)* to the number that are not *(n-r)*. This is algebraically equivalent to the ratio of the percentage prevalence *P* to *100-P* or to the proportional prevalence *p* to *1-p*. Thus, although the dependent variable is a proportion *p*, the linear model is fitted, using the method of maximum likelihood, on the scale of $y = log(p/(1-p))$ known as the logistic transformation of *p*. Because of this distances on the scale are differences of the form *log(odds2) - log(odds1)* which are the logarithms of *'odds ratios'* i.e. *log(odds 2/odds 1)*.

As a consequence of this the anti-logarithms of the logistic regression coefficients give the odds ratio for two risks one unit apart on the scale of that independent variable. The estimation process provides a standard error *(se)* for each regression coefficient so, assuming that the sampling distribution of the estimated coefficient is Normal, which is reasonable for large data sets, coefficients which are more than two se's from zero can be taken to indicate variables genuinely associated with changes in the proportions from which the *'log(odds) y variable'* was obtained. For the analyses presented in this text coefficients more than 2 se's from zero (equivalent to *p<0.05*) have been indicated with the symbol * and on occasion, when they are mentioned in the text, coefficients more than 1.64 se's from zero (equivalent to *p<0.01*) have been indicated with the symbol *?*.

When several factors are being considered at one time there are many ways in which they might interact. The effects of factor A may depend on the level of factor B which generates a two factor interaction. If these two factor interactions change according to the levels of factor C we have a three factor interaction and so on for 4, 5 and higher level interactions. If such interactions are found, then the pattern of relationships will be complicated and the analysis will not permit a simple description. If, on the other hand, the interactions can be assumed negligible then the estimated parameters give the change in the *log(odds)* of the prevalence associated with a change in level cf the particular factor whatever the levels of other factors. Models without interactions are known as Main Effect (ME) models. A complete analysis must first test for interactions. Only if they are absent does it make sense to interpret the main effects model.

The appropriate strategy is to fit the model with all two factor interactions and then the main effects model. If the model including the interactions fits the data little better than the simpler model then that is evidence that interactions are not required. The fit of a least squares regression model is measured by the residual variation about the model. Different models are compared using the residual sums of squares to perform F tests.

In the case of models fitted using Maximum Likelihood the fit is measured by the deviance, so named by Nelder and Wedderburn (1972). For a given model this is calculated as *-2log(maximum_likelihood)* which means that the difference between two deviances is the classic Likelihood Ratio test statistic (Kendall and Stuart, 1961). With the sample sizes as large as in this study this statistic has a distribution very close to the chi-squared distribution. This means that models can be compared using the differences in their deviances as approximate chi squared tests. In a comparison of a model containing two factor interactions and one containing main effects only the difference between the two deviances is an overall chi squared test of all the two factor interactions. If it is not significant and there are no strikingly large interaction parameters, then it is reasonable to assume the main effects model to be an adequate description of the patterns in the data and the next step is to interpret it. Of course the absence of two factor interactions does not totally exclude the possibility that there are higher order interactions, but it is generally safe to proceed on that assumption.

3.7 'Survival' Curve Analysis

It would be useful to be able to assess how various factors are related to the age at which a child takes up smoking. If the associations found represent causal relationships that can be manipulated then in theory a means of delaying uptake could be deduced. However, as is common with data concerned with when events occur over time, the data on age at uptake are censored. That means that for some individuals the age at uptake is only known to be less than or greater than some value. The standard methods for dealing with this type of data if the censoring is all of the second type is known as survival data analysis.

The name arises because the approach was first developed for investigations of mortality in one or more groups because age at death is rarely known for all subjects. The methods were originally developed as descriptive techniques to produce what are called 'Life tables' from which survival curves can be plotted. These curves show the estimated proportion surviving against time since some defined starting point such as date of diagnosis. As for incidence, the effects of various factors on survival can be assessed using regression modelling techniques based on maximum likelihood methods (Cox; 1982). The curves can be converted to plots of the percentage 'not surviving', or in this case 'having tried smoking', by subtracting the ordinates from 100%. In cases such as this the curve is more easily interpretable in this form since it indicates the total uptake at each point in time and the slope of the curve indicates the rate of uptake.

Because the event is not death, but the transition from non-smoker to smoker it is necessary to define what is meant by smoker and to realise that using these methods the transition once made has to be considered permanent. This means that we are investigating what factors are associated with the act of taking up smoking for the first time. This obviously has to ignore the subsequent smoking history of individuals who do take it up, but for current purposes this is a minor restriction.

The methods cannot directly use the data from those children who had started smoking before they entered the study. These children have to be omitted and the analysis restricted to those children classified as non-smokers in 1974. However the curves can then be adjusted to obtain the curve appropriate for all children. This gives the total uptake and the rate of uptake for all children over the range of ages considered.

3.8 Attributable Fractions

For the purpose of designing Anti-smoking programmes it is not only necessary to identify factors associated with the uptake of smoking, but also to assess the magnitudes of the effects on future smoking prevalences that might be achieved by altering them. Of course this requires that to some extent the relationship is causal. Whether or not an association between, for example, parental smoking and childrens smoking is causal or not is difficult to establish. It requires intervention studies, at least, demonstrating that changing such a factor is almost invariably followed by reductions in incidence before one could confidently assume causality. In this study all we can do is assess, assuming some specified degree of causality, how much effect an anti-smoking programme might have on incidence.

To investigate this, we need to use the 'Population Attributable Fraction' concept from classical epidemiology (Last 1983). This is defined as the fraction of 'cases' of disease in a population due to a particular risk factor. In the current context we are not concerned with a disease, but a pattern of behaviour. A case is defined as a child who smokes. If we take mothers smoking as the risk factor then, assuming causality, the fraction of all the children who smoke who do so due to exposure to a smoking mother is the 'population attributable fraction'. It is these children who, in theory, would be prevented from smoking if all mothers could be persuaded to give up the habit.

21

The Attributable Fraction in the population is

$$AF_p = \frac{p_{exp}(p_e/p - 1)}{1 + p_{exp}(p_e/p - 1)}$$

where p_{exp} is the proportion of the population exposed p is the risk if not exposed and p_e is the risk if exposed.

In practice this is generally expressed in terms of the relative risk

$$RR = p_e/p$$

or the odds ratio

$$OR = \frac{p_e/(1-p_e)}{p/(1-p)}$$

when

$$AF_p = \frac{p_{exp}(OR(1+p(OR-1))-1)}{1+p_{exp}(OR(1+p(OR-1))-1)}$$

Finally and most conveniently for current purposes the attributable fraction can be written as

$$AF_p = \frac{p_{exp}(p_e - p)}{p_t}$$

where p_t is the total population prevalence.

This can also be written as

$$AF_p = \frac{p_{exp}(p_e - p)}{p_{exp} \cdot p_e + (1-p_{exp})p}$$

3.9 Allowing for Other Factors

This procedure could be applied to each factor in turn to assess how much effect altering it might have. However, using the raw data in this way ignores the fact that observed differences could be the composite result of several factors. It also ignores the fact that a health education program, to be efficient, should be aimed at modifying several factors at the same time. To take this into account it is necessary to fit a regression model identifying the way in which the associated factors are separately and together related to variation in the prevalence of smoking. The logistic regression coefficients can then be used to obtain odds ratios which for specified population subgroups can be used to obtain attributable fractions appropriate to the factors.

However, the factor of interest will often be associated with other factors which are in turn associated with an increased risk of smoking. Calculations of the attributable fraction using the raw figures are comparing the prevalences of the exposed and unexposed averaged over the various subgroups defined by the other factors. Logistic regression models, on the other hand, are firstly linear on the logistic i.e. log-odds scale and secondly identify for individuals in each factor level category how they differ, on average, from those in a base category with all factors at level 1. They provide odds ratio for the 'exposed' v 'unexposed' adjusted for the effects of other factors. Unfortunately the attributable fraction calculations require not only the odds ratio, but also the prevalence in the 'unexposed'. This means that it is necessary to specify which particular pair of 'exposed' and 'unexposed' categories are to be compared and to identify their make-up with respect to the other factors. Only then can the prevalence be deduced and the population attributable fraction calculated.

One solution is to consider the group of individuals with all factors, except the one of interest, at a particular specified level. This defines a sub-population for whom a prevalence estimate can be obtained and the attributable fraction calculated. However in that case the result will apply only to that subgroup of the population. A more general approach is required which also allows estimation of what proportion of smokers in the population are the result of exposure to a single risk factor or a combination when several risk factors are operating simultaneously.

The only option open in practice is to take the available sample as representative of the population of interest. The sample then determines the make up of the population in terms of the proportions exposed to the different risk factors separately and in combination. A logistic regression model considered to fit the data adequately can then be used to determine the overall proportions of individuals that would have been smokers if the proportions exposed to the various risk factors could be altered in particular ways. From these the fractions, of individuals smoking, attributable to different risk factors or combinations of risk factors can be obtained.

In most of the analyses each individual has been entered as a separate observation. Thus for the given set of covariates or factor levels there is one individual at risk (i.e. a binomial denominator of 1) and zero or 1 individuals positive (i.e. a binomial outcome variable of 0 or 1). This is in contrast to the traditionally more common situation where individuals with the same covariate and factor levels are first grouped, but it is perfectly acceptable and gives the same results (Swan; 1986). Thus to obtain an overall fitted prevalence it is necessary to estimate from the model the risk for each individual given his or her covariate and factor levels. These are then summed over all individuals in the sample to get the fitted number of positives. This divided by the number in the sample gives the total prevalence estimated from the model. Using the data as it was when the model was fitted this process gives an overall prevalence identical to that observed. However, if all individuals in a particular risk category have their factor levels changed to mimic moving them out of that risk category and the process repeated an overall prevalence reduced by the fraction attributable to that risk factor is obtained. Thus by a process of modifying the data in various ways and obtaining the overall prevalences predicted by the model for the modified data we can deduce the appropriate attributable fractions of risk. The practical application of these techniques is illustrated more fully in the results section.

4 Results

4.1 The Sample

A total of 6330 children and 6197 parents returned questionnaires in 1974, but only 5789 of those from the parents matched responding children and not all were complete. For this reason the numbers available for each analysis vary. In particular this affects analyses using data from the parents' questionnaires since they required information to be provided by both the child and the mother and sometimes the father as well.

The main characteristics of the sample are summarised in Table 2. The sexes are represented almost equally with 49% boys and 51% girls. It is not possible to compare the social class distribution with that of the population in general. This is because although the General Household Survey (OPCS;1977) gives figures separately for the social class distribution of heads of households when there is a child between 0 and 15 years, it uses a socio-economic classification which does not correspond to the registrar general's six social class categories. The 1970-72 Occupational Mortality Decennial supplement(OPCS;1978) gives the distribution of married women 15-64 years old according to their husbands social class. This approaches the right population for comparison, but families with children of 11-12 years will obviously have a younger age distribution than this group.

Characteristics of the sample at entry in 1974

	N	%
Males	3097	49.0
Females	3228	51.0
Total	6325	
Social Class:		
I	309	5.8
II	879	16.6
III NM	348	6.6
III M	2691	50.7
IV	681	12.8
V	186	3.9
Students	5	<.1
Forces	207	3.9
Total	5306	
Living with:		
Both parents	5293	90.0
Mother only	416	7.1
Father only	99	1.7
Foster parents	15	0.3
Other	56	1.0
Total	5879	
Parent's questionnaire completed by:		
Mother/female gdn	4070	71.3
Father/male gdn	1613	28.3
Other	24	0.4
Total	5707	
Size of Household:		
2 and 3	2494	42.7
4 and 5	2458	42.0
6 and 7	685	11.7
8 and 9	167	2.9
10 or more	37	0.6
Total	5841	
Smoker in the household		
No	1961	33.1
Yes	3961	66.9
Total	5922	
Parents Smoking:		
Neither	1786	30.5
Mother alone	751	12.8
Father alone	1374	23.5
Both	1939	33.1
Total	5850	

The distribution are in fact quite similar except that IIIm is proportionately less common in the older national population i.e. 39.6% compared with 50.7% for the study parents.

It appears that about 9% have moved up to IIInm and II which represent 11.3 and 20.2% compared with 6.6 and 16.6% in the study parents. The remainder appear to have moved down to social class IV. The majority of children were living with both parents although nearly 9% came from single parent families. Most households had between 2 and 5 members with a small proportion (14.6%) of larger families and a few very large 'households' which were probably institutions of some kind. Although not all the children were living with both parents they were often able to report on their smoking habits. Among these parents the prevalence of smoking was 56.6% in the fathers and 46.0% in the mothers. This means that 69.5% of children are exposed to at least one smoking parent and 33.1% are exposed to two smoking parents. It can also be seen that 27.3% of the children are exposed to smoking siblings.

4.2 Response Rates

The children were contacted on seven separate occasions and their parents twice. There were therefore nine separate opportunities for non-response of one sort or another. Table 3 summarises the degree to which the main forms of non-response occurred. There were a small number of refusals and children lost due to absence from school at the start of the study, but 6311 (85.5%) of the 27383 expected in the 11-12 year old entry to the 48 schools completed questionnaires in the first year. Of the parents whose children completed questionnaires in that year 5789 (91.7%) responded, although a number of their questionnaires were incomplete and only 5427 (86.0%) of the possible 6311 child parent pairs were obtained.

Table 3:

Response rates[1] for selected combinations of years and sources (only those children answering the smoking question are considered to have responded)

```
 1974       1975 1976 1977   1978      1981 1984
Child Parent  Child Child Child Child Parent  Child  Child     Number  %Response

 x                                                          6311    85.5
           x                                                6575    83.5
               x                                            6533    83.0
                   x                                        6116    77.7
                       x                                    5615    71.3
                           x                                5610    71.2
                               x                            4737    60.2
 x--------x                                                 5427    86.0
 x--------------x                                           5236    83.0
 x------------------------------------x                     4392    69.6
 x----------------------------------------x                4402    69.8
 x----------------------------------------------x          3738    59.2
 x-------x------------------------ x                        3890    61.6
 x-------x--------------------------------x                 3941    62.4
 x-------x------------------------------------- x           3387    53.7
 x--------------x------x                                    4435    70.3
 x--------------x------x------x                             3626    57.5
 x--------------x------x------x------ x                     2959    46.9
 x-------x------x----- x----- x------ x                     2657    42.1
 x-------x------x----- x----- x------ x-----x              2167    34.3
 x------------------------------------x---------x          3414    54.1
 x------------------------------------x--------- x         2957    46.9
 x-------x--------------------------- x-----x              3033    48.1
 x------------------------------------x---------x------x   2673    42.4
 x-------x--------------------- x-----x----------x         2256    35.7
 x--------------x------x------x------ x---------x-----x     1869    29.6
 x-------x------x----- x----- x------ x---------x-----x    1718    27.2
 x-------x------x----- x------ x-----x--- x-----x          1506    23.9
```

[1]Response rates for the first two single years are calculated as a proportion of those in the class lists of the schools involved who could have responded. There

were 7383 eligible for the study in 1974 of whom 6311 (85.5%) responded with adequate data to be included. Approximately 490 extra children entering the secondary school system in the second year were considered eligible to join the study. This meant a total of 7874 available of whom 6575 (83.5%) responded. For the single years 1976-1984 the denominator is taken as 7874. For longitudinal combinations the rates are calculated as a proportion of those responding on the first occasion in the sequence.

Taken as a proportion of the target sample of 7383 children the 5427 child parent pairs responding was only 73.5%. However since information on parents smoking was also collected from the children, only data on social class was unique to the parents questionnaire. This meant that only the analyses involving social class were necessarily restricted by this.

During the five school years although they responded at least once there was the possibility of the children not responding in any combination of the five. The table indicates what proportion of children were obtained with the complete sequences years 1 and 2, years 1,2 and 3 and so on up to five complete years (83.0,70.3,57.5 and 46.9% respectively). This indicates a steadily decreasing response, inevitable since even if a child reappears after missing a year they cannot be counted as a responder if a complete sequence of questionnaires is required. This illustrates an inevitable shortcoming of longitudinal studies requiring complete data sequences but which cannot ensure complete follow-ups. Fortunately for the aims of this study it is almost as useful to consider the subsets of individuals present in specified pairs of years. Of particular interest are the pairs 1974/78 and 1974/84 for which we have 69.6% (4392) and 59.2% (3738) responses respectively.

The possible bias that might be introduced into the analyses by differential non-response is discussed in the methods section. It is reasonably clear that the cohort prevalences will become progressively less reliable as estimates of the likely prevalence in children of the same age. For this reaon they must be interpreted with considerable caution. Fortunately the comparisons internal to the cohort required to identify factors associated with prevalence and incidence are less sensitive to bias from this source.

4.3 Initial Findings in 1974 when the Cohort was 11-12 years Old

4.3.1.Characteristics at entry

The final sample of 6311 responding children who also answered the smoking questions consisted of 3086 (48.9%) boys and 3225(51.1%) girls. Their parents smoking according to social class is given in Table 4.

Percentage of parents with particular smoking habits by social class

		Social Class					
		I	II	III NM	III M	IV	V
Ever smoked	Father	68.2	69.6	73.7	79.5	84.5	70.6
Cigarettes	Mother	37.4	41.5	45.5	44.6	52.1	41.4
Smokes cigarettes	Father	33.6	40.3	44.3	59.9	62.6	55.6
now	Mother	25.3	29.0	32.0	43.0	42.1	41.8
Pipe or Cigars	Father	23.8	23.7	25.4	21.1	15.0	14.4
Nmin[1]		305	863	341	2609	660	180

General Household Survey 1974

Socio-economic group		1	2	3	4	5	6
Current	Male	29	46	45	56	56	61
Smokers	Female	25	38	38	46	43	43

[1]Not all the parents responded to questions on smoking so the denominators in a particular column may vary. The number quoted is the minimum value used.

There is a clear gradient in prevalence across the social classes. This is similar to that seen in the results from the General Household Survey (OPCS;1977) for the different, although closely related, socio-economic groups.

The distribution of children according to the types of school they were attending are given in Table 5. The largest proportion of the children in the sample, 57.8%, came from comprehensive schools, with 24.3%,11.5% and 6.4% from secondary, grammar and middle schools. However although school effects may be important and have been the subject of a separate paper (ref) they are not the main emphasis here. The problems of making comparisons allowing for the effects of 48 schools are discussed below.

Table 5:

Distribution of children by school type and sex

School Type (1974)	No. of Schools	*No. of Respondents*	
		Male (%)	Female (%)
Grammar	7	342 (11)	389 (12)
Secondary	18	705 (23)	835 (26)
Middle	3	220 (7)	183 (6)
Comprehensive	20	1831 (59)	1830 (57)

The activities and attitudes of the children in the sample are illustrated in Table 6.

Table 6:

Distributions of children in 1974 by activities and attitudes[1]

Activity/Attitude		*Boys* Frequency	%	*Girls* Frequency	%
Evenings doing	None	337	11	235	7
homework	One/Two	1109	36	1098	34
	Three	1630	53	1885	59
Number of	None	227	7	356	11
evenings out	One/Two	840	27	1393	43
	Three	2019	65	1470	46
Spare Time Activities:					
Sports or Games	No	761	25	1577	49
	Yes	2338	75	1654	51
Cinema	No	2295	74	2665	82
	Yes	804	26	566	18
Scouts or Guides	No	2646	85	2634	82
	Yes	453	15	597	18
Music/Hobby	No	1670	54	2070	64
	Yes	1429	46	1161	36

Table 6 contd...

Dancing	No	2967	96	2530	78
	Yes	132	4	701	22
TV/Records	No	806	26	706	22
	Yes	2293	74	2525	78
Mess around	No	1347	43	1792	55
	Yes	1752	57	1439	45
Youth Club	No	2512	81	2581	80
	Yes	587	19	650	20
Boy/Girl friend	No	2659	86	2805	87
	Yes	440	14	426	13
Part time job	No	2598	86	2906	91
	Yes	435	14	276	9
Played Truant	Never	2536	82	2973	93
	Once/Twice	415	14	212	7
	Often	123	4	29	1

Attitudes- Agrees with:

Parents stricter than teachers about smoking	No	1323	43	1455	46
	Yes	1727	57	1736	54
Fed up with school	No	1827	60	2299	72
	Yes	1230	40	902	28
Cigarettes should be harder to get	No	637	21	609	19
	Yes	2426	79	2599	81
Smoking is a dirty habit	No	854	28	804	25
	Yes	2197	72	2398	75
Smoking only bad if a lot:	No	1462	48	1742	55
	Yes	1589	52	1454	45
Parents don't allow me to smoke	No	718	24	734	23
	Yes	2325	76	2448	77
N minimum/maximum		3033/3099		3182/3231	

[1]Because children did not always respond to all questions the number of answers available for a particular question vary.

Children for the most part seem to be quite active doing homework and 'going out'. The boys seem slightly less likely than the girls to spend three or more evenings a week doing homework (53% and 59%) and slightly more likely to go out three or more evenings (65% and 46%). Relatively small proportions were involved in organised social activities such as scouts and guides (15% and 18%) or youth clubs (19% and 20%). However over 70% spent time watching or playing records. Only a small proportion had boy or girl friends (14% and 13%) or a part-time job (14% and 9%). Boys were more likely to admit to truancy than girls (18% and 8%) and 4% of the boys admitted to frequent truancy.

The majority of the children appeared, at this age, to have 'sensible' attitudes. Most were not 'fed-up with school', they predominantly agreed that 'smoking is a dirty habit' and that 'cigarettes should be harder to get'. The majority (>76%) reported that their parents did not allow them to smoke and more than 50% felt that their parents were stricter than the teachers about smoking.

The distribution of children according to the smoking behaviour and attitudes of their parents are given in Table 7.

Table 7:

Distributions of children according to
parental and sibling behaviour and attitudes

Family behaviour and Attitudes		Boys Frequency	%	Girls Frequency	%
Father smokes	Yes	1702	56	1696	53
cigarettes	No	1220	40	1354	42
	D/K	35	1	37	1
	No father	102	3	126	4
Mothers smokes	Yes	1402	46	1453	45
cigarettes	No	1611	52	1712	53
	D/K	30	1	22	1
	No Mother	34	1	34	1
Sibling smoking:					
No siblings		225	7	249	8
Non-smoking siblings		1974	64	2152	67
Sister smokes cigarettes		268	9	252	8
Brother smokes cigarettes		410	13	336	10
Sister and brother smoking		221	7	240	7
N minimum/maximum		3059/3097		3213/3228	

33

Table 7 contd...

Mother's attitudes:

Smoking is a					
dirty habit	No	835	29	845	28
	Yes	2051	71	2133	72
Wouldn't like					
children to smoke	No	2646	92	2710	91
	Yes	236	8	267	9
Shouldn't prevent					
others smoking	No	1476	52	1470	50
	Yes	1382	48	1479	50

| N minimum/maximum | | 2858/2886 | | 2949/2978 | |

Father's attitudes:

Smoking is					
a dirty habit	No	839	33	884	33
	Yes	1734	67	1775	67
Wouldn't like					
children to smoke	No	2363	92	2449	92
	Yes	212	8	213	8
Shouldn't prevent					
others smoking	No	1389	54	1427	54
	Yes	1182	46	1231	46

| N minimum/maximum | | 2571/2575 | | 2658/2662 | |

It appears that more than 53% of children have smoking fathers, more than 45% have smoking mothers and more than 25% have smoking siblings. There is clearly considerable exposure to the activity and possibly to the materials and products of smoking.

It is important to remember that the parents smoking behaviour as reported by the children is not identical to that reported by the parents. Table 8 shows how the two sources of information compare.

Table 8:

Comparison of parent's and children's reports of parental[1] smoking

| | | 'Do you smoke cigarettes now'? | | | |
| | | Fathers Response | | Mothers Response | |
		No	Yes	No	Yes
Boys response to:					
Does your father	No	960	96		
Smoke cigarettes?	Yes	103	1237		
	Don't know	14	5		
		1077	1338		
Boys response to:					
Does your mother	No			1363	43
smoke cigarettes?	Yes			171	975
	Don't know			18	8
				1552	1026
Girls response to:					
Does your father	No	1045	122		
smoke cigarettes?	Yes	108	1215		
	Don't know	14	6		
		1167	1343		
Girls response to:					
Does your mother	No			1456	42
smoke cigarettes?	Yes			156	1014
	Don't know			13	5
				1625	1061

[1]Children without a particular parent have been omitted from the tables involving that parent.

There are obvious discrepancies, but in 91% of cases the children agreed with their fathers response and in 92% of cases with their mothers. The discrepancies may result from various forms of over- or under-reporting.

It is not possible to identify which response is the most reliable, but it seems reasonable to take the children's response in the analyses. The reasons for this are that it seems unlikely that children are knowingly misreporting their parents behaviour and it is really their perception of parental behaviour that matters. If they report a parent as smoking when that parent smokes so occasionally as to think 'it does not count' the child has still seen a smoking parent. If the parent smokes out of sight of the children then the opposite is true. In either case the child's view seems more relevant. Consequently in all the following analyses where a parental smoking variable is used it has been constructed from the responses on the children's questionnaire.

4.3.2 Smoking behaviour at 11-12 years

Smoking among children of this age is relatively limited and the questions asked were phrased accordingly (Appendix I). The distribution of children according to their responses to the smoking question are given in Table 9. Each response has been used to define a category of smoker for future reference and these are given in parentheses.

Table 9:

1974 smoking behaviour of 11-12 year olds by sex

Smoking category	Boys	Girls
I have never smoked a cigarette (Non-smoker)	45.1	60.0
I have only tried smoking once (Experimental smokers)	34.7	28.4
I have smoked sometimes, but I do not smoke as much as one a week (Occasional smokers)	14.2	9.1
I usually smoke between one and six cigarettes a week (Light smokers)	3.1)	1.8)
I usually smoke more than six cigarettes a week (Regular smokers)	)) 6.0) 2.9)	)) 2.5) 0.7)
N	3086	3225

This shows that 6.0% of the boys and 2.5% of the girls regularly smoke more than one cigarette a week by age 11-12 years. 54.9% of the boys and 40.0% of

36

the girls have tried at least one cigarette by this age and only 45.1% of boys and 60.0% of girls had never smoked at all.)

The analyses are concerned with identifying the factors associated with differences in the prevalence of smoking so it is necessary to define precisely what is meant by smoking. For this young age group, children who claim to smoke 1 or more cigarettes per week have been classed as smokers and the rest as non-smokers (i.e. those responding 4 and 5 to question 4 in the 1974 questionnaire - Appendix I). These are the 'Regular Smokers' and 'Light smokers' of Table 9. A number of analyses were repeated with those responding 3 (the 'Occasional smokers') included as smokers. These resulted in much the same conclusions regarding which factors were associated with the habit, which showed that the precise definition of 'smoker' is not crucial and the results obtained not very sensitive to where the dichotomy is made.

The way in which smoking prevalences vary according to a number of other characteristics is summarised in Table 10.

Table 10:

1974 Prevalence of smoking >1 per week by selected characteristics

		Boys (3087)		Girls (3224)	
		N	Prevalence of smoking	N	Prevalence of smoking
Father Smokes	Yes	1695	7.9	1692	3.1
Cigarettes	No	1218	3.5	1352	1.7
	D/K	34	2.9	37	2.7
	No father	102	7.8	125	1.6
Mothers Smoking	Yes	1396	8.2	1452	3.9
	No	1606	4.2	1706	1.2
	D/K	29	3.5	22	0.0
	No Mother	34	5.9	34	5.9
Sibling smoking:					
No siblings		223	2.2	249	0.8
Non-smoking siblings		1970	2.6	2147	1.3
Sister smokes cigarettes		266	10.5	250	6.0
Brother smokes cigarettes		408	13.2	336	4.5
Sister and brother smoking		218	20.6	239	8.4

Table 10 contd...

Evenings doing homework:

	None	336	11.3	234	4.3
	One or Two	1102	7.5	1096	3.7
	Three or More	1628	3.8	1881	1.6

Number of Evenings out:

	None	226	2.2	354	0.3
	One or Two	840	3.3	1391	1.6
	Three or More	2009	7.5	1470	3.8

Spare Time Activities

Sports or Games	No	756	9.9	1572	2.9
	Yes	2331	4.7	1652	2.1
Cinema	No	2284	5.5	2658	2.2
	Yes	803	7.4	566	3.7
Scouts or Guides	No	2636	6.3	2629	2.6
	Yes	451	4.0	595	1.9
Music/Hobby	No	1660	6.9	2065	3.0
	Yes	1427	5.0	1159	1.6
Dancing	No	2955	6.1	2524	2.2
	Yes	132	11.4	700	3.6
TV/Records	No	802	8.0	704	2.6
	Yes	2285	5.3	2520	2.5
Mess around	No	1341	4.0	1788	1.3
	Yes	1746	7.6	1436	4.0
Youth Club	No	2502	4.6	2575	1.6
	Yes	585	12.0	649	5.9
Boy/Girl friend	No	2649	4.8	2799	1.6
	Yes	438	13.0	425	8.5
Part time job	No	2589	5.2	2901	2.3
	Yes	432	10.7	274	4.0

Table 10 contd...

Played Truant	Never	2529	3.4	2968	1.7
	Once or				
	Twice	412	13.4	210	9.5
	Often	121	34.7	29	31.0
Attitudes:					
Parents stricter					
about smoking	Disagree	1318	8.0	1452	2.9
than teacher	Agree	1720	4.5	1733	2.1
Fed up with school	Disagree	1824	1.9	2296	1.5
	Agree	1221	10.5	899	4.8
cigarettes should					
be harder to get	Disagree	632	19.5	607	6.3
	Agree	420	2.4	2595	1.5
Smoking is a	Disagree	847	15.8	802	6.6
dirty habit	Agree	2193	3.8	2393	1.1
Smoking only bad					
if a lot	Disagree	1458	2.7	1741	1.3
	Agree	1583	8.8	1448	3.9
Parents don't	Disagree	715	10.1	731	4.2
allow me to smoke	Agree	2317	4.7	2445	1.9
Mother's attitudes:					
Smoking is a	Disagree	778	7.6	797	2.0
dirty habit	Agree	1873	5.1	1977	2.4
Wouldn't like	Disagree	213	8.5	240	3.3
children to smoke	Agree	2441	5.6	2532	2.2
Shouldn't prevent	Disagree	1284	5.2	1402	1.9
others smoking	Agree	1367	6.4	1373	2.8
Father's attitudes:					
Smoking is a	Disagree	787	5.5	832	1.9
dirty habit	Agree	1598	5.6	1670	2.2
Wouldn't like	Disagree	197	6.1	203	3.0
children to smoke	Agree	2190	5.5	2303	2.1
Shouldn't prevent	Disagree	1099	5.4	1231	1.9
others smoking	Agree	1283	5.6	1336	2.2

The prevalences are low so it is unwise to conclude much from the observed 18 differences without the more searching regression analyses reported later. However, there are signs that parental smoking has an effect. There are also indications albeit based on small numbers, that the absence of a parent is associated with increased smoking. Sibling behaviour seems to have an even stronger association with smoking in both sexes.

As far as activities are concerned smoking appears to be positively associated with 'going out' going to the cinema, dancing, 'messing around' spending time at a youth club or with a boy or girlfriend, having a part-time job and with playing truant. Smoking appears to be negatively associated with 'doing homework', playing sports or games, scouts or guides, spending time on music or a hobby and watching TV or playing records.

Smoking also appears to be negatively associated with the child perceiving their parents as stricter about smoking than the teacher, not being 'fed-up with school', agreeing that 'cigarettes should be harder to get', that smoking is a 'dirty habit' and that parents don't 'allow me to smoke'. Those that agree that 'smoking is only bad if you smoke a lot' appear three times as likely to smoke as those that do not agree or 'don't know'. Parental attitudes do not seem to be associated with children's behaviour very much although there is a suggestion that the children of parents who do not seem to mind if they smoke do smoke more.

Clearly factors such as parental smoking and parental attitude are associated with each other. To determine the separate and independent effects on children's smoking requires the use more of complex analyses the results of which are reported in section 4.3.3.

4.3.3 Factors associated with smoking at 11-12 years

The data available on factors potentially associated with the children's smoking cover their home environment, their social behaviour together with their own and their parents' attitudes. The children's replies to the questions under these headings have, in a number of cases been grouped to form composite variables or factors. The precise definitions of these are given in Appendix II. Table 11 shows how the prevalence of smoking differs according to the different levels of these factors

1974 Prevalences of smoking >1 per week by selected factors

Factors	Category	*Boys*		*Girls*	
		N	% Smokers	N	% Smokers
Parental Smoking	1 Neither	848	2.6	934	1.2
behaviour (PSM)	2 Mother	351	5.1	400	3.0
	3 Father	680	6.0	688	1.5
	4 Both	968	9.4	966	4.2
Sibling smoking	1 No siblings	223	2.2	249	0.8
behaviour (SBS)	2 None smoking	1970	2.6	2147	1.3
	3 At least				
	one smoker	892	14.2	825	6.1
Companions (COM)	1 No friends	362	2.8	565	0.7
	2 Friends of				
	same sex	2106	4.9	1793	1.0
	3 Boy and girl				
	friends	547	12.4	812	6.8
Organised Social	1 Not involved	1926	4.5	1874	1.8
activities (ACO)	2 Involved	1161	8.4	1350	3.5
Unorganised Social	1 Not involved	988	2.6	1295	1.0
Activities (ACD)	2 Involved	2099	7.6	1929	3.5
Sports and	1 Not involved	756	9.9	1572	2.9
games (SPG)	2 Involved	2331	4.7	1652	2.1
Truants	1 Never	2941	4.8	3178	2.2
	2 Sometimes	121	34.7	29	13.0
Part-time job	1 None	2589	5.2	2901	2.3
	2 Has one	432	10.6	274	4.0
Perceived parental					
attitude to	1 Permissive	442	12.4	463	4.5
smoking (PCN)	2 Restrictive	2559	4.8	2682	2.1
General Parental	1 High	1765	4.5	1983	2.0
Concern (PPM)	2 Low	1291	8.1	1219	3.2
Sees positive					
reasons for	1 No	1986	1.3	2239	0.6
smoking(FSM)	2 Yes	1079	14.6	970	6.7

Table 11 contd...

Sees positive reasons against smoking(ASM)	1	No	246	29.3	194	12.4
	2	Yes	2814	3.9	3019	1.8
Childrens beliefs about smoking (HAZ)	1	Realizes hazards	1115	2.2	1455	1.3
	2	Rejects hazards	1946	8.2	1753	3.4
Peer pressure to smoke (PER)	1	Low	1543	0.7	1932	0.5
	2	High	1518	11.3	1275	5.5
Attitude to school (ASC)	1	Satisfied	1447	2.1	1958	1.0
	2	Dissatisfied	1611	9.4	1251	4.7

The effect of parental smoking is even more pronounced when the children of parents who both smoke can be compared with those with only one or no smoking parents. It appears that a very large number of children were exposed to two smoking parents, 968 boys (34%) and 966 girls (32%) and they were three times more likely to be smoking >1 per week than children with non-smoking parents. The sibling behaviour has been compressed into a three category variable for later analysis, but the pattern seen in Table 10 is still clear. Children with any smoking sibling are much more likely to be smokers themselves. The COM factor is designed to summarise information on the nature of the childrens social life. It appears those with a social life involving children of both sexes (COM=3) were also considerably more likely to be smokers.

Overall smoking was positively associated with involvement in both organised 21 and unorganised social activities, truancy, part-time jobs, perceived parental permissiveness to smoking and low general concern for the childs schooling and future. It was also positively associated with the child agreeing that there were positive reasons for smoking, not seeing the hazards as relevant to him or herself, with reported peer pressure and dissatisfaction with school. It was negatively associated with involvement in sports and games, parents who were restrictive with respect to smoking and with the child agreeing with anti-smoking attitudes.

Although several of the factors appear to have quite strong associations with smoking they are also associated to some extent with each other. This means that a factor with a genuine association may well generate an apparent association with other factors. There is also the possibility that the form of an association between smoking and a particular factor actually differs according to the level of another factor. For example the effect of parental smoking on the child's smoking behaviour may well differ for boys and girls.

To estimate the separate and combined effects of these variables on the prevalence of smoking it is necessary to use regression methods. Since the outcome variable in this case is a proportion the appropriate form is logistic regression (Breslow and Day 1980).

The use and interpretation of logistic regression is conveniently illustrated by an analysis involving only the two factors parental smoking and sex. Table 11 showed how the prevalence of smoking varied with these two factors and Figure 3 shows a plot of the prevalence against parental smoking accompanied by the output from a logistic regression using the data from that table.

Figure 3:

1974 % prevalence of smoking >1 per week by parental smoking and sex

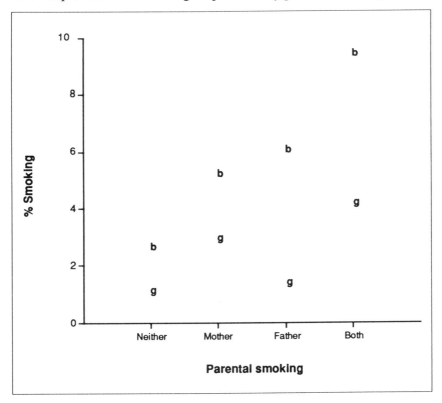

Logistic regression to estimate the effects of sex and parental smoking on the prevalence of 11-12 year old smoking

$fit sex+psm $dis e $

scaled deviance = 3.7304 at cycle 3
d.f. = 3

	estimate	s.e.	parameter	
1	-4.507	0.2014	1	
2	0.9190	0.1422	SEX(2)	*
3	0.8026	0.2568	PSM(2)	*
4	0.7040	0.2269	PSM(3)	*
5	1.344	0.1980	PSM(4)	*

scale parameter taken as 1.000

From the plot it is clear that the boys have higher prevalences than the girls and there is also an effect of parental smoking.

The fitted model estimates both the average difference between the sexes which is the vertical separation of the two sets of proportions and the effects of parental smoking which are seen as deviations from the horizontal, assuming them to be the same for both sexes.

For this analysis the boys' have been coded 2 so the parameter SEX(2), estimated as +0.919 on the log odds scale, indicates how, on average, the boys' prevalence exceeds that of the girls. Since the estimate is more than six times its standard error it is obviously much more than could easily occur by chance. The odds ratio (OR) describing how much more likely the boys are to be smokers than are the girls is exp(0.919) = 2.51 with an approximate 95% confidence interval of exp(0.919-0.1422) = 2.17 to exp(0.919+0.1422) = 2.89. Since the prevalences are quite low (about 2%) the odds ratio is a reasonable approximation to the relative risk (RR).

This means that the boys are estimated from this sample to be 2.5 times as likely as girls to be smoking 1 or more cigarette a week at this age.

The above model assumes that there is no interaction between the factors sex and parental smoking i.e. that the parental smoking effects are the same in both sexes. If this were completely so the two sets of prevalences in Figure 3 would follow more or less parallel lines. In fact although they are not very far from it they are clearly not parallel. The departure from parallelism can be tested with the deviance which, can be taken as an approximate Chi-squared test of whether this sample gives evidence of such an interaction in the population it represents. The number of degrees of freedom is 3 because there are initially 8 prevalences which may vary and a 5 parameter model has been fitted. This leaves 3 degrees of freedom for the data to vary about the model due either to random sampling variations or to the effects of factors or interactions neglected by the model. Thus the approximate chi-squared value is 3.73 with 3df, and since the 95% significance level of Chi-squared with 3 degrees of freedom is 7.81, the slight suggestion that the effects differ does not reach anywhere near the conventional level of significance.

In practice, it is usual to fit a model including 'interactions' i.e. one that allows the parental smoking effects to differ in the two sexes, as well and compare how well it fitted with the simpler model. The more complex model includes interaction parameters which describe precisely how the parental smoking effects in the girls differed from those in the boys.

Figure 4 shows the GLIM output from the model incorporating the appropriate interaction terms.

Figure 4:

Logistic regression of 11-12 year old smoking by parental smoking and sex including interactions

$fit sex+psm+sex.psm $dis e $

scaled deviance = 0.00000000 at cycle 5
d.f. = 0

	estimate	s.e.	parameter
1	-4.430	0.3033	1
2	0.8042	0.3724	SEX(2)
3	0.9536	0.4218	PSM(2)
4	0.2132	0.4398	PSM(3)
5	1.314	0.3427	PSM(4)
6	-0.2459	0.5321	SEX(2).PSM(2)
7	0.6660	0.5158	SEX(2).PSM(3)
8	0.04639	0.4198	SEX(2).PSM(4)

scale parameter taken as 1.000

Because this model requires 8 parameters there are no degrees of freedom to assess variation about the model, it fits the data exactly and has a deviance of zero. However, the parameters representing the interaction between sex and parental smoking have standard errors and, with caution, can be used to assess the likelihood of a genuine interaction in the population represented by this sample.

It seems that the only interaction term larger than its standard error is the SEX(2).PSM(3). This indicates that the effect of the father alone smoking is greater on the boys than it is on the girls. However it would need to reach at least twice its se to be significant and it may well be a chance observation. It has been discussed here to illustrate the interpretation of interaction parameters in such regression models.

In theory this approach can be used to disentangle the effects of all the social, environmental and attitudinal factors on 11 year old smoking. In practice, however, the number of factors involved in this data set is too large to do this. Some selection process has to be used to reduce the number of factors in the regression anlayses to a manageable level. This has been done by taking items of information such as attitudes to the hazards of smoking and compressing responses from several questions into one variable which in the case of the attitudes to hazards has been called HAZ. A complete list of the composite variables used in the analysis with their definitions are given in Appendix II. As an illustration the definitions for those used in this analysis are listed below. In addition a sequence of regressions showed that once a basic set of variables were included in the model the effects of the others diminished to insignificance. This meant that the analyses could be restricted to a manageable subset of the original variables.

The regression analyses reported here are those involving the basic set of variables which are:

SEX   -   1 for males and
                2 for females
SC74   - Social class of the parents in 1974
                1. For I, II and IIInm
                2 for IIm, IV and V
                3 for unknowm
PSM   - Parental smoking in 1974
                1. Neither
                2. Mother
                3. Father
                4. Both

SBS   - Sibling smoking
        1 No siblings
        2. Non-smoking siblings
        3. Smoking siblings
COM   - Companionship: With whom do you spend MOST of your time?
        1. Alone or with parents
        2. Same sex friends
        3. Opposite sex friends
ACS   - Social activities
        1. No more than one of five social activities
        2. Two or more of the five
PER   - Peer pressure:
        Three attitude statements indicated susceptibility
        to peer pressure to smoke
        1. Did not agree two any of three
        2. Agreed with at least one of the three
HAZ   - Awareness of hazards of smoking:
        Three attitude statements implied that hazards only apply
        to the old, to the long term or to the heavy smokers.
        1. Did not agree to any of the three
        2. Agreed to one or more of the three

With this many factors there are obviously many possible interactions and they cannot be assumed negligible without some investigation as outlined in the methods section. The model fitted to explain variation in the prevalence of 11-12 year old smoking with these factors and all the two factor interaction terms is shown in Figure 5.

Figure 5:

Regression analysis of 1974 smoking on selected factors plus two factor interactions

$FIT (SEX+SC74+PSM+SBS+COM+ACS+PER+HAZ).
    (SEX+SC74+PSM+SBS+COM+ACS+PER+HAZ)$DIS E $

SCALED DEVIANCE = 3974.3 AT CYCLE 5
        D.F. = 6101   FROM 6187 OBSERVATIONS

contd. overleaf

Figure 5: contd.

	ESTIMATE	S.E.	PARAMETER	
1	-6.224	1.277	1	
2	-1.057	0.5712	SEX(2)	
3	0.7506	0.7406	SC74(2)	
4	0.8481	0.8224	SC74(3)	
5	0.5114	0.8789	PSM(2)	
6	0.6561	0.7874	PSM(3)	
7	0.6619	0.7381	PSM(4)	
8	1.655	1.184	SBS(2)	
9	2.911	1.201	SBS(3)	
10	1.635	1.135	COM(2)	
11	2.001	1.204	COM(3)	
12	1.229	0.6109	ACS(2)	
13	2.634	0.5603	PER(2)	
14	0.4654	0.6015	HAZ(2)	
15	0.3514	0.2564	SEX(2).SC74(2)	
16	0.3005	0.2832	SEX(2).SC74(3)	
17	0.7196	0.2908	SEX(2).PSM(2)	*
18	0.2046	0.2643	SEX(2).PSM(3)	
19	0.4967	0.2402	SEX(2).PSM(4)	*
20	-0.5038	0.3650	SC74(2).PSM(2)	
21	-0.2461	0.3296	SC74(2).PSM(3)	
22	0.2880	0.3225	SC74(2).PSM(4)	
23	-0.1702	0.4001	SC74(3).PSM(2)	
24	0.04566	0.3865	SC74(3).PSM(3)	
25	0.1577	0.3655	SC74(3).PSM(4)	
26	-0.3166	0.4269	SEX(2).SBS(2)	
27	-0.3860	0.4284	SEX(2).SBS(3)	
28	0.1180	0.5421	SC74(2).SBS(2)	
29	-0.2802	0.5553	SC74(2).SBS(3)	
30	-0.3787	0.6122	SC74(3).SBS(2)	
31	-0.1624	0.6199	SC74(3).SBS(3)	
32	0.1472	0.6597	PSM(2).SBS(2)	
33	0.08229	0.6686	PSM(2).SBS(3)	
34	0.05944	0.6035	PSM(3).SBS(2)	
35	0.2465	0.6125	PSM(3).SBS(3)	
36	-0.3439	0.5423	PSM(4).SBS(2)	

contd. overleaf

Figure 5: contd.

37	-0.2681	0.5480	PSM(4).SBS(3)
38	0.2404	0.3010	SEX(2).COM(2)
39	0.6081	0.3216	SEX(2).COM(3)
40	-0.4788	0.4743	SC74(2).COM(2)
41	-0.8354	0.5000	SC74(2).COM(3)
42	-0.2724	0.5141	SC74(3).COM(2)
43	-0.4709	0.5446	SC74(3).COM(3)
44	-0.5344	0.5108	PSM(2).COM(2)
45	-0.4022	0.5454	PSM(2).COM(3)
46	-0.5284	0.4516	PSM(3).COM(2)
47	-0.2591	0.4876	PSM(3).COM(3)
48	-0.2306	0.4344	PSM(4).COM(2)
49	0.02789	0.4631	PSM(4).COM(3)
50	-1.238	1.032	SBS(2).COM(2)
51	-0.7263	1.084	SBS(2).COM(3)
52	-0.9701	1.040	SBS(3).COM(2)
53	-0.7661	1.092	SBS(3).COM(3)
54	-0.1573	0.1828	SEX(2).ACS(2)
55	-0.07309	0.2508	SC74(2).ACS(2)
56	-0.2132	0.2776	SC74(3).ACS(2)
57	-0.07872	0.2949	PSM(2).ACS(2)
58	0.08933	0.2651	PSM(3).ACS(2)
59	-0.3490	0.2422	PSM(4).ACS(2)
60	-0.2966	0.4623	SBS(2).ACS(2)
61	-0.3014	0.4645	SBS(3).ACS(2)
62	0.06923	0.3200	COM(2).ACS(2)
63	0.1150	0.3439	COM(3).ACS(2)
64	-0.1613	0.1744	SEX(2).PER(2)
65	-0.01122	0.2411	SC74(2).PER(2)
66	-0.09979	0.2668	SC74(3).PER(2)
67	-0.3391	0.2833	PSM(2).PER(2)
68	-0.3657	0.2527	PSM(3).PER(2)
69	-0.3718	0.2334	PSM(4).PER(2)
70	-0.3791	0.4222	SBS(2).PER(2)
71	-0.3272	0.4243	SBS(3).PER(2)
72	-0.1303	0.2925	COM(2).PER(2)
73	-0.2635	0.3167	COM(3).PER(2)
74	-0.06935	0.1772	ACS(2).PER(2)
75	-0.1035	0.2014	SEX(2).HAZ(2)

contd. overleaf

76	-0.3378	0.2755	SC74(2).HAZ(2)
77	-0.3494	0.3112	SC74(3).HAZ(2)
78	0.5699	0.3264	PSM(2).HAZ(2)
79	0.2307	0.2831	PSM(3).HAZ(2)
80	0.2567	0.2619	PSM(4).HAZ(2)
81	0.2811	0.4594	SBS(2).HAZ(2)
82	-0.04720	0.4607	SBS(3).HAZ(2)
83	0.3687	0.3289	COM(2).HAZ(2)
84	0.1395	0.3580	COM(3).HAZ(2)
85	-0.1581	0.2092	ACS(2).HAZ(2)
86	0.009648	0.1968	PER(2).HAZ(2)

SCALE PARAMETER TAKEN AS 1.000

The deviance is 3974.3 with 6101 df. The single factor parameters e.g. PSM(3) have no very useful interpretation when the model contains interaction parameters involving them e.g. SEX(2).PSM(3). They only represent differences within the group of individuals with all other factors at level 1.

In this model only the interaction parameters should be considered. In fact we see that of all the interaction terms only SEX(2).PSM(2) and SEX(2).PSM(4) exceed twice their se's

This suggests that when all three factors are taken into account the girls are more affected by their mothers smoking than are the boys. Boys are nearly three times as likely to smoke as the girls unless the mother smokes. When that is the case it appears that the girls are influenced more than the boys and although both become more likely to smoke the boys are now only about 1.5 times as likely to be smokers.

Figure 6 gives the GLIM results for the main effects model with a deviance of 4043.5 and 6173 df. Note the degrees of freedom has increased by 72 because that number of parameters, those representing the two factor interactions, have been dropped from the model. The difference between the two deviances is 69.2 which can be taken as a chi-squared test of the two factor interactions as a whole with 72 df. Since the 95% significance level for chi-squared on 72 df is 92.7, taken as a group, the two factor interactions are far from significant. However the SEX.PSM interactions are in two cases more than twice their standard errors. Making the assumption, reasonable with a sample this size, that the coefficients follow more or less Normal dists this should only occur by chance for 5% of such estimates. Thus there is some evidence that they represent genuine effects.

Figure 6:

Regression analysis of 1974 smoking on selected factors
- main effects model -

$FIT SEX+SC74+PSM+SBS+COM+ACS+PER+HAZ $DIS E $

SCALED DEVIANCE = 4043.5 AT CYCLE 4
           D.F. = 6173   FROM 6187 OBSERVATIONS

	ESTIMATE	S.E.	PARAMETER	
1	-4.079	0.2568	1	
2	-0.6527	0.08305	SEX(2)	
3	-0.07903	0.1130	SC74(2)	
4	-0.01452	0.1253	SC74(3)	
5	0.4153	0.1344	PSM(2)	*
6	0.3787	0.1194	PSM(3)	*
7	0.4382	0.1102	PSM(4)	*
8	0.2515	0.1970	SBS(2)	
9	1.295	0.1987	SBS(3)	*
10	0.2070	0.1387	COM(2)	
11	0.8121	0.1503	COM(3)	*
12	0.5713	0.08468	ACS(2)	*
13	1.700	0.08209	PER(2)	*
14	0.6608	0.09393	HAZ(2)	*

SCALE PARAMETER TAKEN AS 1.000

The main effects model in Figure 6 gives the estimated effects of the various factors allowing for the others. In the case of SEX and PSM the effects are averages of effects shown to be different in the interaction model so they must be interpreted cautiously. The other effects can be interpreted as differences expected whatever the levels of the other factors. For example SBS(3) = 1.295 indicates that, all else equal, children with smoking siblings are $\exp(1.295) = 3.65$ times as likely to be smokers than those children of this age without siblings (the reference group SBS=1). Because 1.295 is more than 6 times its se (0.1987) it is highly significant. In fact all the factors in the model, except social class (SC74) have significant effects. It appears that once the other factors such as parental smoking are taken into account there is no difference in the prevalence of 11-12 year old smoking between the social classes. On

51

average parental smoking puts up the prevalence by a factor of about 1.7 to 1.9 in the boys and 2.3 to 3.4 in the girls. Boys are about 2.4 to 2.9 times as likely to smoke as girls if their mothers don't smoke and about 1.4 to 1.8 times as likely if the mother does smoke.

The effect of smoking siblings is discussed above. It appears that non-smoking siblings do not affect the likelihood of a child smoking (SBS(2) = 0.25 with se=0.20) neither does spending time with same sex companions compared to spending it alone or with parents (COM(2)=0.21 with se = 0.14). On the other hand spending time with companions of the opposite sex has a highly significant effect COM(3) = 0.81 which is more than 5 times its se of 0.15. These children are more than twice as likely to smoke than those who spend their time alone or with their parents. Children with an active social life are also significantly more likely to be smokers ACS(2) = 0.57 which is 6 times its se of 0.08. The odds ratio exp(0.57) = 1.77. This means that children with an active social life and who spend their time with children of the opposite sex are exp (0.81 + 0.57) = 4.0 times more likely to smoke than children who spend their time alone or with parents and are less socially active.

Finally the PER and HAZ effects were highly significant. Those children who agreed with statements implying they felt peer pressure proved much more likely to be smokers (OR=5.5). Those children who appeared unaware of the hazards of smoking were 1.9 times as likely to be smokers.

The prevalence of smoking varied quite considerably from one school to another. Since the characteristics in the model above are not equally represented in each school there is a possibility that they are confounded with school effects. To investigate this the above analysis was repeated with a 48 level school factor. This showed that there were systematic school differences which may partly represent the effects of the ways in which the schools are run, their local regulations on smoking and so on. However there also seem to be cultural group differences which lead to quite marked changes in prevalence from school to school which are otherwise quite similar.

The effects of school characteristics have been presented and discussed in an earlier publication (Murray, Kiryluk and Swan 1984). In the regression model allowing for these school differences the associations already seen in figure 5 and discussed above are thrown into sharper focus. Their directions and magnitudes remain relatively unchanged, but their standard errors are considerably reduced so they become much more significant in the statistical sense. It is clear that the school effects are not distorting the estimation of the other factor effects.

It appears that although the prevalence is low at this age strong associations are already to be found with a number of factors. Insofar as these factors can be modified by health education and consequently produce reductions in prevalence or incidence subsequent to that age they are pointers to how health education programs should be designed. How these factors are actually associated with subsequent incidence is dealt with in later sections. It is now necessary to consider the association of smoking and other factors with the children's respiratory health at this age.

4.4 Findings in 1978 when the Cohort was 15-16 years Old

4.4.1 Smoking behaviour at 15-16 years

In the fifth year of the study only 69.6% of the original entry could be contacted. The percentage dropout rate by 11-12 year old smoking categories are given in Table 12.

Table 12:

1978 Response rates by 11-12 year old smoking category

1974 Smoking category	Boys		Girls	
	N	%	N	%
Non-smokers	1392	71.8	1935	75.2
Experimental smokers	1073	69.4	916	66.5
Occasional smokers	437	59.5	293	64.8
Light smokers	97	58.8	57	49.1
Regular smokers	88	48.9	23	52.2

There is clearly an association between smoking behaviour and the likelihood of responding or being available to respond as argued earlier in the methods section. However this will not greatly affect analyses relying on internal comparisons Although it must be carefully considered in the interpretation of results.

Table 13 shows the numbers of boys and girls according to their responses to the 1978 smoking question.

Table 13:

1978 Smoking behaviour of 15-16 year olds by sex

Smoking Category	Boys	Girls
I have never smoked a cigarette (Non-smokers)	24.9	29.3
I have only tried smoking once (Experimental smoker)	27.9	24.0
I have smoked sometimes but I do not smoke as much as one a week (Occasional smokers)	8.7	9.8

Table 13 contd...

I usually smoke between one and six cigarettes a week (Light smokers)	4.4	5.9
I usually smoke more than six cigarettes a week (Regular smokers)	21.4	17.4
I used to smoke but I have given it up (Ex-smokers)	12.7	13.6
Numbers available	2700	2915

Notice that there is now a category of ex-smokers. The prevalence of regular smoking (more than 1 a week) which in 1974 was 6.0% in the boys and 2.5% in the girls has risen to 25.8% and 23.3% respectively. Although many of the children's characteristics altered during the four years of the study from the first to the fifth questionnaire, the primary interest is to assess what characteristics at age 11-12 years are associated with the development of later smoking. For that reason, although contemporaneous factors may well be associated more strongly with 1978 smoking, Table 14 gives the 1978 15-16 year old prevalences of regular smoking for boys and girls classified according to various factors as they applied in 1974.

Table 14:

1978 Prevalences of smoking >1 per week by 1974 factors

1974 Factors	Category	N	*Boys* % Smokers	N	*Girls* % Smokers
Parental Smoking	1 Neither	617	16.7	732	15.6
behaviour (PSM)	2 Mother	259	23.6	277	19.1
	3 Father	473	23.9	498	22.1
	4 Both	606	31.2	628	29.9
Sibling smoking	1 No siblings	164	18.9	205	18.0
behaviour (SBS)	2 None smoking	1406	19.3	1583	19.1
	3 At least one smoker	537	38.5	507	34.1
Companions (COM)	1 No friends	266	14.3	409	14.7
	2 Friends of same sex	1453	22.4	1296	19.7
	3 Boy and girl friends	345	38.0	552	34.4

Table 14 contd...

Organised Social	1 Not involved	1332	20.9	1350	17.6
activities (ACO)	2 Involved	776	29.8	947	28.9
Unorganised Social	1 Not involved	698	17.8	933	16.1
Activities (ACD)	2 Involved	1410	27.4	1364	26.5
Sports and	1 Not involved	500	25.8	1096	22.3
games (SPG)	2 Involved	1608	23.7	1201	22.3
Truants	1 Never	2042	23.4	2272	22.0
	2 Sometimes	52	53.8	15	60.0
Part-time job	1 None	1790	22.8	2090	21.0
	2 Has one	284	32.4	177	35.6
Perceived parental attitude to	1 Permissive	304	27.0	322	25.2
smoking (PCN)	2 Restrictive	1751	23.9	1929	21.8
General Parental	1 High	1206	21.6	1428	20.3
Concern (PPM)	2 Low	882	28.0	855	25.5
Sees positive reasons for	1 No	1395	18.2	1638	18.6
smoking(FSM)	2 Yes	701	36.1	652	31.7
Sees positive reasons against	1 No	157	48.4	133	36.1
smoking(ASM)	2 Yes	1931	22.3	2158	21.5
Childrens beliefs OC about	1 Realizes hazards	786	17.6	1084	17.2
smoking (HAZ)	2 Rejects hazards	1304	28.3	1205	26.9
Peer pressure	1 Low	1121	16.9	1445	18.1
to smoke (PER)	2 High	968	32.6	844	29.6
Attitude to school	1 Satisfied	1043	18.2	1449	17.1
(ASC)	2 Dissatisfied	1045	30.3	842	31.2

More or less the same patterns observed in 11-12 year old prevalences (Table 11) are seen again and in some cases in a much more pronounced form. The effect of the parental smoking as reported in 1974 still appears very clear even though parental smoking decreased by about 4% between 1974 and 1978.

One parent smoking was associated with an increase in the prevalence of 7% in the boys and 5% in the girls and both parents smoking was associated with an increase in prevalence from about 15% to 30%. The effect of siblings is also clear. Non-smoking siblings have no apparent effect, but a smoking sibling is associated with increases of about 18%.

Children who in 1974 spent their time with companions of the opposite sex, took part in organised and unorganised social activities appeared more likely to smoke than those who did not do this although being involved in sports and games appeared not to be associated with smoking behaviour. Those who reported 'truanting' or a part-time job in 1974 were very much more likely to be smoking regularly in 1978 although the number of children involved was quite small.

Children who in 1974 had seen their parents as permissive about smoking or unconcerned in general were slightly more likely to be smoking in 1978 than those who had not. If they had reported seeing positive reasons for smoking or dismissed positive reasons against smoking in 1974 they were considerably more likely to be smoking in 1978 than those who had not. Finally those children who had been dismissive of the hazards involved in smoking or who had agreed with statements implying they were susceptible to peer pressure on smoking were also considerably more likely to be smoking regularly in 1978 than those who had not.

Table 15 and 16 show the equivalent figures for the boys and girls separately according to their 1974 smoking behaviour. Thus the 1978 prevalences in the children who were non-smokers in 1974 are the incidences between 1974 and 1978.

Table 15:
1978 Prevalences of smoking >1 per week by 1974 factors (boys)

| 1974 Factors | Category | N | 1974 Smoking | | | |
			Non-Smokers	Experi-mental	Occ-asional	Regular >1/week
	Total	2099	10.0	28.6	48.5	71.7
			(1002)	(745)	(260)	(92)
Parental Smoking	1 Neither	615	8.5	19.0	47.5	69.2
behaviour (PSM)	2 Mother	259	9.1	28.2	56.0	70.0
	3 Father	471	10.6	28.7	38.7	71.0
	4 Both	604	11.4	36.1	55.1	72.7

Table 15 contd...

Sibling smoking	1	No siblings	163	9.8	30.6	44.4	66.7
behaviour (SBS)	2	None smoking	1404	9.6	24.4	43.9	65.6
	3	At least one smoker	532	11.9	38.0	53.8	75.4
Companions (COM)	1	No friends	264	9.3	20.3	25.0	20.0
	2	Friends of same sex	1448	9.6	26.5	46.9	76.9
	3	Boy and girl friends	343	10.2	40.0	60.0	71.4
Organised Social	1	Not involved	1326	9.1	27.6	43.9	69.6
activities (ACO)	2	Involved	773	12.1	30.1	52.6	73.9
Unorganised Social	1	Not involved	694	9.0	25.3	35.8	71.4
Activities (ACD)	2	Involved	1405	10.7	30.0	51.7	71.8
Sports and	1	Not involved	497	7.4	29.3	48.3	72.5
games (SPG)	2	Involved	1602	10.7	28.4	48.5	71.2
Truants	1	Never	2033	9.8	28.5	46.5	71.3
	2	Sometimes	52	23.1	33.3	76.5	80.0
Part-time job	1	None	1783	9.9	27.4	44.3	80.9
	2	Has one	282	10.5	35.5	65.9	47.8
Perceived parental attitude to	1	Permissive	301	10.9	21.9	49.1	82.6
smoking (PCN)	2	Restrictiv	1745	10.0	29.6	49.0	69.1
General Parental	1	High	1201	8.9	28.1	45.2	70.0
Concern (PPM)	2	Low	878	11.7	29.5	52.8	73.1
Sees positive reasons for	1	No	1389	8.2	27.2	40.5	53.8
smoking(FSM)	2	Yes	698	15.5	31.5	55.4	74.7
Childrens beliefs about smoking (HAZ)	1	Aware of hazards	785	8.1	26.2	42.6	75.0
	2	Rejects hazards	1296	11.6	30.0	50.5	71.3

Table 15 contd...

Peer pressure	1 Low	1118	8.2	26.0	51.6	62.5
to smoke (PER)	2 High	962	13.8	31.2	47.7	72.6
Attitude to school	1 Satisfied	1040	8.0	26.8	44.3	72.2
(ASC)	2 Dis-satisfied	1039	12.9	30.4	50.8	71.6

Table 16:

1978 Prevalences of smoking >1 per week by 1974 factors (girls)

1974 Factors	Category	N	*1974 Smoking*			
			Non-smokers	Experi-mental	Occ-asional	Regular >1/week
	Total	2293	13.3 (1455)	33.7 (609)	44.7 (190)	71.8 (39)
Parental Smoking	1 Neither	730	10.0	27.9	40.0	62.5
behaviour (PSM)	2 Mother	270	11.8	23.1	47.8	57.1
	3 Father	497	14.6	28.7	45.2	100.0
	4 Both	628	15.6	47.0	43.6	72.2
Sibling smoking	1 No siblings	205	12.2	32.4	50.0	50.0
behaviour (SBS)	2 None smoking	1580	12.2	30.7	41.1	75.0
	3 At least one smoker	506	19.9	39.9	47.8	70.6
Companions (COM)	1 No friends	408	10.5	26.6	41.7	50.0
	2 Friends of same sex	1294	12.7	32.7	42.1	55.6
	3 Boy and girl friends	551	20.3	37.5	47.5	81.5
Organised Social	1 Not involved	1348	10.6	29.6	46.8	63.6
activities (ACO)	2 Involved	945	18.1	38.2	43.2	75.0
Unorganised Social	1 Not involved	930	10.5	31.7	42.1	33.3
Activities (ACD)	2 Involved	1363	15.8	34.5	45.4	75.0
Sports and	1 Not involved	1094	11.8	36.9	46.4	64.7
games (SPG)	2 Involved	1199	14.6	30.7	43.0	77.3
Truants	1 Never	2268	13.3	33.4	44.0	68.6
	2 Sometimes	15	0.0	50.0	60.0	100.0

Table 16 contd...

Part-time job	1 None	2087	13.0	32.2	41.8	72.7
	2 Has one	176	15.8	43.9	60.7	66.7
Perceived parental attitude to smoking (PCN)	1 Permissive	321	14.3	32.4	42.9	70.0
	2 Restrictive	1927	12.8	34.1	45.8	72.4
General Parental Concern (PPM)	1 High	1426	13.1	32.8	37.5	72.2
	2 Low	853	13.3	35.5	50.5	71.4
Sees positive reasons for smoking(FSM)	1 No	1637	11.6	34.0	37.5	80.0
	2 Yes	649	19.6	33.3	50.0	70.6
Children's beliefs about smoking (HAZ)	1 Aware of hazards	1084	12.5	26.7	38.3	80.0
	2 Rejects hazards	1201	14.2	38.2	46.5	69.0
Peer pressure to smoke (PER)	1 Low	1445	12.2	32.5	38.3	80.0
	2 High	840	16.0	35.2	48.1	70.6
Attitude to school (ASC)	1 Satisfied	1447	10.8	29.6	42.6	77.8
	2 Dissatisfied	840	19.3	39.2	45.9	70.0

Clearly the smoking behaviour in 1974 is highly predictive of smoking in 1978. Over 70% of those smoking regularly in 1974 were still doing so, about 44% of those classed as occasional smokers in 1974 had become regular smokers as had about 25% of those classed as experimental smokers in 1974. Of the non-smokers only about 10% had become regular smokers in 1978.

It seems that the effects of factors such as parental and sibling smoking appear in two forms in these tables. They are associated with the 1974 smoking and they appear to be associated to varying degrees with the maintenance of regular smoking from 1974 to 1978 and with the rate of conversion from occasional or experimental smoking in 1974 to regular smoking by 1978.

The relationship of parental and sibling smoking with the incidence of regular smoking in those not smoking in 1974 is not so marked. There is some suggestion of a positive association but the differences are of the order of 2% and insufficient to confirm a real association. The associations between the factors must be allowed for to increase the sensitivity of the analysis if genuine associations of this order are to be identified.

How these factors relate to each other and are associated with prevalence and incidence is considered below in the model fitting analysis.

4.4.2 Factors identified at ages 11-12 years associated with smoking at 15-16 years

Because the sexes might differ in a number of ways the regression analyses were performed separately for boys and girls. Figure 7 gives the output from a set of logistic regressions relating variation in 1978 smoking prevalence to factors representing the children's characteristics in 1974.

Figure 7:

Regression analysis of 1978 prevalence of smoking
on 1974 characteristics

Boys

$FIT (SC74+PSM+SBS+COM+ACS+PER+HAZ).
(SC74+PSM+SBS+COM+ACS+PER+HAZ) $

scaled deviance = 1994.4 at cycle 4
d.f. = 1977   from 2050 observations

$FIT SC74+PSM+SBS+COM+ACS+PER+HAZ $DIS E $
scaled deviance = 2072.4 at cycle 4
d.f. = 2037   from 2050 observations

	estimate	s.e.	parameter	
1	-2.412	0.2925	1	
2	-0.06168	0.1406	SC74(2)	
3	0.2578	0.1590	SC74(3)	
4	0.3396	0.1758	PSM(2)	
5	0.3012	0.1547	PSM(3)	
6	0.4914	0.1452	PSM(4)	*
7	-0.09757	0.2180	SBS(2)	
8	0.5771	0.2292	SBS(3)	*
9	0.1581	0.1745	COM(2)	
10	0.6871	0.2065	COM(3)	*
11	0.3120	0.1132	ACS(2)	*
12	0.6682	0.1176	PER(2)	*
13	0.3773	0.1201	HAZ(2)	*

scale parameter taken as 1.000

Girls

$FIT (SC74+PSM+SBS+COM+ACS+PER+HAZ).
(SC74+PSM+SBS+COM+ACS+PER+HAZ) $

scaled deviance = 2138.0 at cycle 4
d.f. = 2190   from 2263 observations

$FIT SC74+PSM+SBS+COM+ACS+PER+HAZ $DIS E $

scaled deviance = 2197.8 at cycle 4
d.f. = 2250   from 2263 observations

	estimate	s.e.	parameter	
1	-2.473	0.2586	1	
2	-0.1236	0.1363	SC74(2)	
3	-0.06909	0.1611	SC74(3)	
4	0.1811	0.1731	PSM(2)	
5	0.2581	0.1499	PSM(3)	
6	0.5629	0.1393	PSM(4)	*
7	0.1046	0.2021	SBS(2)	
8	0.6062	0.2169	SBS(3)	*
9	0.1330	0.1605	COM(2)	
10	0.5709	0.1818	COM(3)	*
11	0.5141	0.1159	ACS(2)	*
12	0.6329	0.1222	PER(2)	*
13	0.3243	0.1114	HAZ(2)	*

scale parameter taken as 1.000

For each sex the first fitted model, for which the parameter estimates have not been printed includes all possible two factor interactions. The deviance from this model compared with the deviance from the main effects model in the figure gives a test of all these interactions as a group. The test uses the difference between the deviances as an approximate chi-squared test of all the interactions as a group. For the boys the difference between the deviances is 78.0 with 2037-1977 = 60 df. For the girls the eqivalent chi-squared test is 59.8 also on 60 df.

Since the 95th centile for chi-square with this many degrees of freedom is 79.0 the interactions as a group are no greater,for either sex, than could easily occur by chance. It is not necessary to include the interactions in the model and the main effects model can be taken as an adequate representation of the data.

The main effects model for the boys, Figure 7, appears to show that once parental and sibling smoking is taken into account the social class groups do not differ. Both parents smoking in 1974 appears to be strongly associated with the 15-16 year old boys prevalences of smoking since both PSM(4) coefficients are more than three times their standard errors. Similar positive associations are seen for smoking siblings, opposite sex companions, social activities, peer pressure and disregard for the hazards of smoking. Peer pressure in particular is 6 times its standard error and boys who showed themselves as susceptible to it in 1974 are, on average $\exp(0.7413) = 2.1$ times as likely to be smoking at the age of 15-16 years as those that did not. The pattern among the girls is very similar with all the same associations significant and those with parental and sibling smoking tending to be slightly more pronounced as if girls were susceptible to the same influences and at the same time more sensitive to them.

This analysis has ignored the information available on the 1974 smoking habits. The 1974 smoking behaviour could be included in the model as a factor, but that may not be appropriate. Later smoking among those classified as non-smokers or triers in 1974 represents the rate at which those children have taken it up. For those classified as occasional or regular smokers in 1974 later smoking rates represent the extent to which they have maintained the habit. Analysing all these groups together means assuming incidence and maintenance are influenced by the same factors in the same way. If only the non-smokers in 1974 are used in the analysis the fitted parameters are estimates of the effects of the factors on the incidence of smoking between 1974 and 1978. This is probably the most important analysis because it is the largest group (56%) and more than 25% of the later smokers arise from it. In addition children in this group are the least advanced along the road to smoking and should therefore be the most easy to deter with appropriate health education programs. The 'triers' in 1974 make up 31% of the children and produce 41% of the later smokers. Analysis of this group is also concerned with the incidence of later regular smoking. However, the factors related to variation in this incidence and their patterns of association could be quite different to those associated with incidence among total non-smokers. The analyses of the other two groups could be considered as assessing what factors influence children who are already smoking to some degree, to give it up. Figures 8 and 9 give the outputs from models fitted separately for these four 1974 smoking groups for the boys and girls respectively.

Regression analysis of 1978 smoking for separate
1974 smoking categories (boys)

Boys
Non-smokers in 1974

$FIT SC74+PSM+SBS+COM+ACS+PER+HAZ $DIS E $

scaled deviance = 617.74 at cycle 4
d.f. = 961   from 974 observations

	estimate	s.e.	parameter	
1	-2.386	0.4712	1	
2	-0.08020	0.2707	SC74(2)	
3	0.1450	0.3206	SC74(3)	
4	-0.03874	0.3613	PSM(2)	
5	0.1982	0.2902	PSM(3)	
6	0.1338	0.2876	PSM(4)	
7	-0.1061	0.3610	SBS(2)	
8	0.02308	0.4320	SBS(3)	
9	-0.2925	0.2770	COM(2)	
10	-0.4693	0.4260	COM(3)	
11	0.3288	0.2264	ACS(2)	
12	0.5977	0.2796	PER(2)	*
13	0.3839	0.2255	HAZ(2)	

scale parameter taken as 1.000

Experimental smokers in 1974

$FIT SC74+PSM+SBS+COM+ACS+PER+HAZ $DIS E $

scaled deviance = 832.25 at cycle 4
d.f. = 717   from 730 observations

	estimate	s.e.	parameter
1	-1.515	0.4675	1
2	-0.07840	0.2191	SC74(2)

3	0.2279	0.2454	SC74(3)	
4	0.5094	0.2717	PSM(2)	
5	0.6541	0.2446	PSM(3)	*
6	0.8203	0.2325	PSM(4)	*
7	-0.3709	0.3381	SBS(2)	
8	0.1941	0.3550	SBS(3)	
9	0.02443	0.2778	COM(2)	
10	0.7264	0.3296	COM(3)	*
11	0.006382	0.1772	ACS(2)	
12	0.001085	0.1927	PER(2)	
13	0.1263	0.1813	HAZ(2)	

scale parameter taken as 1.000

Occasional and regular smokers in 1974

$FIT SC74+PSM+sbs+COM+ACS+PER+HAZ $DIS E $

scaled deviance = 448.29 at cycle 4
d.f. = 333   from 346 observations

	estimate	s.e.	parameter	
1	-1.697	0.8078	1	
2	0.1169	0.3020	SC74(2)	
3	0.3390	0.3340	SC74(3)	
4	0.6549	0.4031	PSM(2)	
5	-0.1147	0.3228	PSM(3)	
6	0.4226	0.3028	PSM(4)	
7	-0.06916	0.6247	SBS(2)	
8	0.2924	0.6257	SBS(3)	
9	1.090	0.4358	COM(2)	*
10	1.473	0.472O49	COM(3)	*
11	0.05115	0.2445	ACS(2)	
12	0.3076	0.2439	PER(2)	
13	0.1054	0.2988	HAZ(2)	

scale parameter taken as 1.000

65

Figure 9:

Regression analysis of 1978 smoking for separate
1974 smoking categories (girls)

Girls
Non-smokers in 1974

$FIT SC74+PSM+SBS+COM+ACS+PER+HAZ $DIS E $
scaled deviance = 1073.6 at cycle 4
d.f. = 1423 from 1436 observations

	estimate	s.e.	parameter	
1	-2.696	0.3505	1	
2	0.02748	0.1974	SC74(2)	
3	0.08201	0.2387	SC74(3)	
4	0.1848	0.2554	PSM(2)	
5	0.3136	0.2139	PSM(3)	
6	0.2896	0.2098	PSM(4)	
7	0.07573	0.2711	SBS(2)	
8	0.5317	0.3113	SBS(3)	
9	0.1412	0.2197	COM(2)	
10	0.4937	0.2698	COM(3)	
11	0.5797	0.1724	ACS(2)	*
12	0.3319	0.2282	PER(2)	
13	0.02169	0.1629	HAZ(2)	

scale parameter taken as 1.000

Experimental smokers in 1974

$FIT SC74+PSM+SBS+COM+ACS+PER+HAZ $DIS E $

scaled deviance = 723.65 at cycle 4
d.f. = 588   from 601 observations

	estimate	s.e.	parameter
1	-1.240	0.4734	1
2	-0.3885	0.2336	SC74(2)
3	-0.2490	0.2755	SC74(3)

4	-0.2812	0.3049	PSM(2)	
5	0.01315	0.2519	PSM(3)	
6	0.7802	0.2344	PSM(4)	*
7	-0.1281	0.3879	SBS(2)	
8	0.1620	0.4043	SBS(3)	
9	0.03677	0.2805	COM(2)	
10	0.2542	0.3099	COM(3)	
11	0.1712	0.1965	ACS(2)	
12	0.4321	0.1981	PER(2)	*
13	0.4816	0.1952	HAZ(2)	*

scale parameter taken as 1.000

Occasional and regular smokers in 1974

$FIT SC74+PSM+SBS+COM+ACS+PER+HAZ $DIS E $
scaled deviance = 304.66 at cycle 4
   d.f. = 213   from 226 observations

	estimate	s.e.	parameter
1	-0.9886	0.9922	1
2	-0.1966	0.4216	SC74(2)
3	-0.4203	0.4536	SC74(3)
4	0.6047	0.4628	PSM(2)
5	0.4137	0.4436	PSM(3)
6	0.3248	0.3958	PSM(4)
7	-0.02413	0.6447	SBS(2)
8	0.2399	0.6514	SBS(3)
9	0.1704	0.5878	COM(2)
10	0.6470	0.6028	COM(3)
11	0.03905	0.3277	ACS(2)
12	0.3154	0.2829	PER(2)
13	0.1370	0.3246	HAZ(2)

scale parameter taken as 1.000

Among the 974 boys who had never smoked (Figure 8(a)) in 1974 there was only one significant association and that was with PER indicating that susceptibility to peer pressure was a predictor of later incidence. The factor HAZ indicating disregard of the hazards was positively associated with incidences as was ACS indicating involvement with social activities, but neither reached significance. There was no significant evidence of a parental smoking effect although the associations with the father and both parents smoking were positive. The 730 boys who, in 1974 had tried smoking only once, showed some evidence that their incidence of regular smoking by 1978 was significantly higher when the father or both parents had been smoking in 1974 and the association with mothers smoking nearly reached significance. Those reporting spending their time with companions of the opposite sex in 1974, COM(3), were also significantly more likely to have started smoking regularly by 1978. The remaining factors did not appear to be associated with the incidence of regular smoking in this group.

Among the 346 boys, who in 1974 were already smoking to some extent those with mothers and both parents smoking were slightly more likely to be smoking regularly in 1978, but these effects did not reach significance. Those who spent their time with the same or opposite sex companions were significantly more likely to be still smoking regularly in 1978. There was also a positive association with susceptibility to peer pressure, but this fell short of significance.

Among the 1436 girls who had never smoked in 1974 there was some suggestion of a parental smoking effect, but it did not quite reach significance. Social activities had a significant effect and there were positive associations with smoking siblings, opposite sex companions and peer pressure, but they did not reach significance. Among the 601 girls who had tried smoking in 1974 the effect of both parents smoking was highly significant with an Odds ratio compared with neither parent smoking of $\exp(0.7802) = 2.18$. The effects of susceptibility to peer pressure and being dismissive of the hazards were significantly positively associated with the incidence of regular smoking in 1978. Among the 226 girls who were to some extent smoking in 1974 the same pattern of associations was seen, but it was not so marked as to reach significance with these small numbers.

4.5 Findings in 1981 when the Cohort was 18-19 years Old

The 1981 survey of the children when most of them had left school was a pilot for a more extensive follow-up study. Because of this the questionnaire was kept very short and restricted to simple questions on smoking habits, occupation and health (see Appendix I). Of the 6983 individuals sent questionnaires (identified from the 1978 school class lists) 413 (5.9%) could not be contacted due to changes of address 1380 (19.8%) were apparently still at the same address but chose not to reply and 5190 (74.3%) actually did respond. Again there was evidence that those who were known to be smoking at an earlier stage were less likely to respond. Table 17 gives the response rates by 1978 smoking categories. Obviously prevalence figures are likely to be biased.

Table 17:

1981 Percentage response rates by 1978 smoking behaviour

1978 Smoking	*Boys*		*Girls*	
category	% response	(N)	%	(N)
Non-Smoker	76.2	(671)	80.9	(857)
Experimental-smoker	79.2	(755)	80.1	(699)
Ex-smoker	72.7	(344)	76.1	(394)
Occasional	79.9	(234)	80.5	(287)
Light and Regular	67.4	(699)	70.7	(675)

There is a slight suggestion that the girls are more ready to respond than the boys and a clearly lower response rate in the light and regular smokers for both sexes. Fortunately investigations of associations by the estimation of odds ratios from comparisons are unlikely to be much affected.

4.5.1 Smoking behaviour in 18-19 year olds

The questions on smoking in the 1981 questionnaire were very brief
i.e.

Do you smoke cigarettes now? .... yes/no
If yes, how many cigarettes do you usually smoke each day?
If no, have you ever smoked regularly
(at least 1 cigarette a day)?........yes/no

Although this was not enough to distinguish between 'Triers' and 'Ex-smokers' there was sufficient information for individuals to be allocated to smoking categories equivalent to those used earlier.

Table 18 gives the distribution of the 18-19 years olds according to their smoking categories by sex.

There is quite a high percentage of non-smokers compared to earlier findings (58.1% of boys and 60.2% of girls), but these include the triers and probably a number who would have been classified as occasional in the earlier results. There are now, at this age, about 30% of the cohort smoking daily and 16.7% of boys and 9.3% of the girls smoking more than 20 a day.

Table 18:

Smoking behaviour as reported in 1981 by sex

	N	*Boys* %	N	*Girls* %
Non-smokers	1572	58.1	1749	60.2
Ex-Smokers	233	8.6	286	9.9
Smokers	902	33.3	868	29.9
< 5/day	60	2.2	109	3.8
5 - 9	60	2.2	88	3.0
10-14	168	6.2	236	8.1
15-19	161	5.9	164	5.6
20+	453	16.7	271	9.3
Total	2707		2903	

Table 19 gives the prevalence of smoking defined clearly in 1981 for each sex according to occupation in 1981 and a number of factors applying in 1978 and 1974.

Table 19:

1981 Prevalence of daily smoking in 18-19 year old boys and girls by current and earlier characteristics

		Boys % N		*Girls* % N	
1981					
Employment status	1. employed	32.7	(1831)	28.2	(1797)
	2. unemployed	51.3	(310)	42.5	(294)
	3. student	16.9	(320)	15.6	(347)
	4. housewife	-	-	43.7	(284)
	5. forces	40.6	(106)	26.3	(19)
Marital status	1. married	52.3	(155)	37.1	(412)
	2. single	32.1	(2464)	28.7	(2395)

Table 19 contd...

1978

Smoking status					
	1. never	6.0	(502)	4.9	(677)
	2. tried once	12.3	(586)	11.7	(545)
	3. <1/week	37.3	(185)	32.0	(222)
	4. 1-6/week	67.5	(80)	59.5	(116)
	5. >6/week	81.3	(380)	81.2	(351)
	6. Ex-smoker	29.9	(244)	26.3	(293)

1974

Parents smoking	1. neither	26.0	(616)	19.7	(694)
(PSM)	2. mother	30.7	(241)	37.4	(275)
	3. father	34.7	(452)	30.7	(488)
	4. both	35.9	(604)	36.4	(634)
Parents social class	1. I,II & IIInm	26.6	518	26.1	545
	2. IIIm, IV & V	33.6	1203	31.4	1307
Attitudes to hazards	1. Aware	24.0	761	23.2	1014
(HAZ)	2. Dismissive	36.6	1260	34.9	1192
1974 Smoking status	1. never	17.8	961	20.2	1393
	2. tried	37.3	721	40.4	617
	3. <1/week	48.4	275	54.3	186
	4. 1-6/week	72.7	66	69.0	29
	5. >6/week	91.7	36	90.9	11

There are about 11-12% of the cohort unemployed and they have much higher prevalences of daily smoking (51.3% compared to 32.7% in the boys and 42.5% compared to 28.2% among the girls). In both sexes those that have married at this age, 18-19 year, smoke markedly more. The prevalences in 1981 are strongly related to their smoking behaviour in 1978 and 1974 and also show some positive association with parental smoking as reported in 1974. The boys appear to be influenced most by the fathers smoking and the girls by that of the mother. There is a slight gradient according to the parents' social class in 1974 with children from manual homes smoking more. How the children responded to the attitude questions on hazards in 1974 appears to be quite predictive of their smoking as 18-19 year olds. Model fitting analyses for smoking in 1981 show associations with 1974 and 1978 characteristics. However, it is the associations with 1984, for which this was a pilot that are of most interest so the 1981 analyses will not be discussed here, but the main findings can be found in Murray et al (1984).

4.6 Findings in 1984 when the Cohort was 21-22 years Old

The questionnaire was designed in the light of a pilot interview survey of 80 members of the cohort in 1982. The questions on smoking were redrafted to be suitable for young adults and a number of questions on work, social life and other activities relevant to young adults were included. Fuller details of this pilot may be obtained from the report to the MRC (ref) and the HEJ papers.

Using the modified address list from the 1981 pilot study 7543 questionnaires were despatched, 1153 (15.3%) were returned by the post office because they could not be delivered due to changes of address and 4778 (63.3%) were returned completed. Table 20 gives the cumulative response rate for each of the four mailings.

Table 20:

Cumulative response rate over four mailings in 1984
(percentages of 7543 sent initially in parentheses)

	Completed returns	Blank returns	Refusals
1st mailing	2817 (37.3)	702 (9.3)	7 (0.1)
2nd mailing	3917 (51.9)	845 (11.2)	9 (0.5)
3rd mailing	4530 (60.1)	1086 (14.4)	28 (0.4)
4th mailing	4778 (63.3)	1153 (15.3)	32 (0.4)

The refusal rate was 0.7% for those reached by a questionnaire and data was obtained from 4737 (75%) of those 6311 children starting the study 10 years before.

4.6.1 Characteristics of the cohort as young adults

The distributions of the cohort as young adults in 1984 age 21-22 years according to their demographic occupational and social characteristics are shown in Table 21.

Over one third of the girls had married by this age which was twice the marriage rate of the boys. The social class distribution shows that the largest proportion of the cohort were in social class III with the girls being predominantly in the non-manual category. In both sexes there were about 14.6% with unknown social class of whom the majority were students.

Unemployment is lower among the girls, but 14.6% described themselves as full-time housewives and they may not all have been seeking paid employment.

Table 21:

Demographic occupational and social characteristics
reported in 1984

	Males (2344)	Females (2424)
Marital Status:		
Single	79.0	60.6
Married	16.6	32.9
Divorced/Separated	1.3	2.9
Not known	3.1	3.6
Social class:		
I	2.3	0.8
II	7.7	11.8
IINM	10.9	38.9
IIIM	39.6	11.1
IV	18.4	20.6
V	6.6	2.3
Not known	14.6	14.6
Employment status:		
Full time job	73.9	60.0
Part time job	1.7	4.1
Housewife	-	14.6
Housewife+job	-	2.0
Unemployed	11.6	7.0
Armed forces	3.2	0.8
Other	9.6	9.1
Go to the pub:		
Never	9.0	16.2
Some/most evenings	91.0	83.8
Play sport:		
Never	40.2	58.7
Some/most evenings	59.8	41.3
Attend classes:		
Never	85.6	79.9
Some/most evenings	14.4	20.1
Alcohol consumption:		
None	6.1	12.9
Little	31.6	48.9
Moderate	48.2	33.2
Quite a lot	11.6	4.5
A lot	2.4	0.5

Among the boys 59.8% claimed to do some sort of sporting activity at least some evenings. This was less common in girls for whom the figure was 41.3%. More girls attended classes (20.1%) than boys (14.4%). Going to the pub at least some evenings was reported by (91.0%) of boys and (83.8%) of the girls. Very few reported consuming no alcohol, 6.1% of boys and 12.9% of girls.

4.6.2 Smoking behaviour in 21-22 year olds

The questions on smoking in the 1984 questionnaire were

Have you ever smoked ? ....Yes/No
If yes: Do you smoke now ? .... Daily/Occasionally/Not at all

there were also several questions on consumption for current and ex-smokers (Appendix I)

From the answers to these questions the young adults were identified as belonging to one of four smoking categories, non-smoker, ex-smoker, light smoker (less than 5/day) and heavy smoker (5 or more a day). The percentage distribution among these categories is given in Table 22.

Table 22:

1984 Smoking behaviour by sex

	Boys	*Girls*
Smoking:		
Smokers ≥5/day	26.7	19.1
<5/day	11.9	13.6
Ex-smoker	13.4	15.9
Non-smoker	48.0	51.4
N	2292	2368

More than a quarter of the young adults were smoking daily (38.6% men and 32.7% women) and about 50% in both sexes were currently smoking or had previously smoked. With smokers at this age defined as those admitting to smoking daily. Table 23 gives the prevalence of smoking according to the young adults characteristics as they were in 1984 and according to their earlier characteristics observed in 1978 and 1974.

Table 23:

1984 Prevalence of daily smoking (%) by current and earlier characteristics

	Males	(N)	Females	(N)
1984:				
Social class				
I,II and III NM	28.6	(497)	28.1	(1219)
IIIM,IV and V	42.5	(1477)	39.6	(793)
Marital status				
Single	36.4	(1787)	34.1	(1457)
Married	43.3	(400)	27.8	(753)
Separated	76.7	(30)	48.5	(68)
Other	53.7	(54)	35.2	(54)
Parental Smoking:				
Mother: No mother	42.1	(76)	34.9	(86)
Non-smoker	35.2	(1286)	28.7	(1385)
Smoker	43.4	(860)	39.8	(827)
Father: No father	40.1	(147)	38.7	(168)
Non-smoker	34.3	(999)	28.1	(1039)
Cigarette smoker	43.6	(869)	37.0	(843)
Pipe/Cigar only	35.5	(197)	33.2	(235)
Employment status:				
Full time job	36.9	(1687)	28.8	(1455)
Part time job	51.3	(39)	32.0	(100)
Housewife	-		37.6	(340)
Housewife/job	-		40.4	(47)
Unemployed	54.8	(261)	47.5	(166)
Forces	34.2	(73)	42.1	(19)
Other/unknown	29.8	(225)	34.4	(232)
Shiftwork:				
No	36.6	(1625)	30.7	(1806)
Yes	46.6	(522)	41.1	(331)
Job satisfaction:				
No	43.0	(635)	37.2	(602)
Yes	36.7	(1492)	30.3	(1480)
Sporting activity:				
Never	46.3	(912)	35.3	(1332)
Some/most evenings	32.7	(1316)	28.6	(976)

Table 23 contd...

1978 Smoking:				
Non-smoker	9.9	(446)	7.2	(573)
Trier	18.5	(513)	17.3	(462)
Ex-smokerl	41.3	(206)	26.5	(245)
occasional	46.3	(162)	42.1	(195)
Regular	81.1	(403)	74.4	(386)
1974/Smoking:				
Non-smoker	22.0	(853)	22.1	(1165)
Trier	45.3	(629)	42.6	(505)
Occasional	56.2	(235)	59.9	(157)
Regular	79.0	(81)	79.5	(44)
Parental smoking:				
Neither parent	33.6	(539)	22.9	(619)
Mother	34.9	(212)	39.0	(236)
Father	40.4	(403)	31.7	(397)
Both	40.1	(529)	39.5	(506)
Aware of hazards				
No	42.1	(1097)	23.9	(986)
Yes	29.6	(699)	37.1	(981)
Perceived peer pressure				
No	30.3	(971)	28.1	(1176)
Yes	45.3	(827)	39.1	(691)

The prevalence of smoking in the males is, overall, higher that in the females. However, Table 23 shows that within the broad social class grouping of Non-manual and manual the smoking prevalences of the sexes were much the same.

Single young men and women had much the same prevalence of smoking (36.4%,34.1%) while the prevalence among married women was rather lower (27.8%) and the prevalence among married men was considerably higher (43.3%). The prevalences among the separated were much higher in both sexes (76.7% and 48.5%).

Both the mothers and the fathers smoking behaviour appears to have an influence in both sexes. The young men had prevalences about 8% higher if a parent smoked. The women with smoking mothers had a prevalence (39.8%) half as large again as those with non-smoking mothers (28.7%). A similar difference was seen between young women with non-smoking and smoking fathers where the prevalences were 28.1% and 37.0%.

Employment status appears to have a strong association with smoking. In particular those unemployed have almost one and a half times the prevalence of those in full time employment in both sexes. Shift work is associated with an increase in prevalence for both sexes.

There was some suggestion that those with less job satisfaction and/or with less involvement in sporting activities were more likely to smoke. Earlier smoking behaviour was highly predictive of their smoking as young adults. Of those smoking regularly more than one a week in 1978 there were 81.1% of the 403 boys and 74.4% of the 386 girls still doing so in 1984. On the other hand those children who reached the age of 15-16years without smoking at all had a low uptake between then and 1984. In the 446 boys in this category the incidence over the five year period was 9.9% and in the 573 girls it was 7.2%.

Consideration of the factors that applied 10 years earlier in 1974 when the children were 11-12 years old shows that their smoking behaviour then was quite predictive of later behaviour as was their parents smoking at that time. Those children whose attitudes showed them to be susceptible to peer pressure and dismissive of the hazards at ages between 11 and 12 years were more likely to be smokers 10 years later.

The magnitudes of the associations between these factors and how they are interrelated will be dealt with in more detail in the discussion of the model fitting analysis below.

4.6.3 Factors associated with Smoking in 21-22 year olds

Figures 10 and 11 give the results of logistic regression analyses, one for each sex, quantifying the associations between a number of factors representing the characteristics, circumstances and attitudes of the cohort in 1984 and ten years earlier in 1974.

Figure 10:

Regression analysis of 21 - 22 year old smoking
by 1984 and 1974 factors

- *Boys*

$FIT EMPS+SC84+SHFT+INJS+SPOR+PS84+
      SC74+PSM+COM+ACS+PER+HAZ $DIS E $

scaled deviance = 1830.8 at cycle 4
d.f. = 1488   from 1512 observations

	estimate	s.e.	parameter	
1	-1.302	0.2460	1	
2	0.9428	0.4448	EMPS(2)	*
3	0.000	aliased	EMPS(3)	
4	0.000	aliased	EMPS(4)	
5	0.6916	0.2002	EMPS(5)	*
6	0.02097	0.4172	EMPS(6)	
7	0.2652	0.2935	EMPS(7)	
8	0.3268	0.1477	SC84(2)	*
9	0.06371	0.3435	SC84(3)	
10	0.4765	0.1326	SHFT(2)	*
11	-0.2361	0.1247	INJS(2)	
12	-0.4235	0.1185	SPOR(2)	*
13	-1.038	0.2665	SPOR(3)	*
14	0.3786	0.2210	PS84(2)	
15	0.1627	0.1703	PS84(3)	
16	0.3686	0.2015	PS84(4)	
17	-0.2883	0.1425	SC74(2)	*
18	-0.1966	0.1772	SC74(3)	
19	-0.3501	0.2285	PSM(2)	
20	0.09383	0.1755	PSM(3)	
21	-0.1161	0.1990	PSM(4)	
22	0.2146	0.1777	COM(2)	
23	0.4622	0.2228	COM(3)	*
24	0.3515	0.1181	ACS(2)	*
25	0.5055	0.1176	PER(2)	*
26	0.2926	0.1228	HAZ(2)	*

scale parameter taken as 1.000

Regression analysis of 21 - 22 year old
smoking by 1984 and 1974 factors

- Girls

$FIT EMPS+SC84+SHFT+INJS+SPOR+PS84+
    SC74+PSM+COM+ACS+PER+HAZ $DIS E $

scaled deviance = 1715.4 at cycle 4
d.f. = 1492 from 1518 observations

	estimate	s.e.	parameter	
1	-1.622	0.2449	1	
2	0.2062	0.2812	EMPS(2)	
3	-0.008233	0.1855	EMPS(3)	
4	0.1329	0.3843	EMPS(4)	
5	0.7557	0.2525	EMPS(5)	*
6	1.961	0.8286	EMPS(6)	*
7	0.4306	0.3289	EMPS(7)	
8	0.3621	0.1299	SC84(2)	*
9	0.6353	0.3849	SC84(3)	
10	0.6549	0.1566	SHFT(2)	*
11	-0.2847	0.1314	INJS(2)	*
12	-0.2418	0.1255	SPOR(2)	
13	-1.472	0.5777	SPOR(3)	*
14	0.4853	0.2212	PS84(2)	*
15	0.2357	0.1747	PS84(3)	
16	0.3064	0.2035	PS84(4)	
17	-0.1735	0.1502	SC74(2)	
18	-0.3182	0.1918	SC74(3)	
19	0.3234	0.2209	PSM(2)	
20	0.2184	0.1868	PSM(3)	
21	0.3653	0.2005	PSM(4)	
22	-0.02677	0.1730	COM(2)	
23	0.5802	0.1975	COM(3)	*
24	0.3422	0.1277	ACS(2)	*
25	0.1699	0.1254	PER(2)	
26	0.2881	0.1246	HAZ(2)	*

scale parameter taken as 1.000

There were a number of very strong associations and the patterns, with minor differences, are much the same in both sexes. Among the 1512 available for this analysis the prevalence of smoking was significantly higher in those employed part-time or not at all. It was significantly higher among those in the manual social class group and in those doing shiftwork. It was significantly lower in those involved in sporting activities. The effects of parental smoking (as reported in 1984) did not quite reach significance once the other factors had been taken into account, but they were not far from it. There was a suggestion that boys who, in 1974, had fathers in the manual social classes were less likely to smoke as young adults, but this is a little difficult to interpret since it has been estimated after adjustment for the effects of the subjects own social class in 1984. Finally those that, at the age of 11-12 years in 1974, had had opposite sex social companions, were involved in social activities, were susceptible to peer pressure or were dismissive of the hazards of smoking were all more likely to be smoking ten years later. These results are considered in more detail in section 4.7.3 in the discussion of Attributable Fractions.

4.7 Further Longitudinal Findings

The regression analyses investigating the relationships between early characteristics and later smoking take considerable advantage of the longitudinal nature of the data. However they do not use the data from intervening years.

There are three approaches to using these data which address slightly different questions. To investigate the pattern of smoking uptake in the cohort as a whole using data from all years until the child starts smoking is possible with lifetable methods and 'survival' curves as discussed in the methods section. This requires that a report of regular smoking, for example, is taken as a 'terminal' event and the probability of an individual 'terminating' by each age obtained. This technique allows the rate at which the cohort takes up the smoking habit to be examined. This approach can be combined with regression methods to assess how much various characteristics are associated with a high rate of taking up smoking.

To investigate the pattern of developing smoking behaviour in the individual child may also be useful. However there is a bewildering array of possibilities for each child and some simplification is necessary for a practical analysis. Here the individual patterns have been classified, using a within subject regression analysis, according to how rapidly those that took up smoking did so. Logistic regression analysis has then been used to identify the factors associated with the risk of a child falling into this category. The third approach is designed to investigate the relative chronology of changes in attitudes and smoking behaviour using data on both these from every year.

Finally the earlier results obtained using logistic regression to identify which early factors are associated with later smoking have been extended to estimate the fractions of the later smoking which can be associated with, and possibly attributed to, these factors either separately or in various combinations. This identifies the magnitude of effects that might be achieved with health education programmes that were aimed at modifying these factors.

4.7.1 'Survival' curve analysis

The analysis in this section uses the data to investigate how long children survive as non-smokers. To use the appropriate life table techniques designed for survival data it is neccessary to define a "terminal event". In order to draw comparisons between the length of "survival" as total non-smokers and the length of "survival" as non- or experimental smokers two definitions of a "terminal event" are used. In the first instance this is defined as the event of a child reporting a single cigarette (i.e. all responses other than "never" to the smoking question) while the second definition requires that the child reports regularly smoking more than one cigarette a week.

Using the first definition of a "terminal event" the children's responses other than "never" to the smoking question may be used to determine the year in which a child reached that event. In turn this information may be used to obtain curves describing the accumulating proportion of children having tried smoking by age. With a first report of regular smoking as the terminal event curves describing the cumulative uptake of regular smoking can be obtained and compared.

Thus the main aim of this section is to investigate the association between a number of 1974 characteristics of the children and the year in which the children

     i) first started smoking *and*
     ii) first started smoking regularly.

This investigation has been restricted to those of the children's 1974 characteristics which persistently gave significant associations in the logistic regression analyses. These are the characteristics represented by the composite variables HAZ, PER and PSM (Appendix II). They represent attitudes to the hazards of smoking and to peer pressure and parental smoking behaviour. The variable PCN has also been included even though it was not found to have a significant effect on prevalence because it is of particular interest from a health education point of view. It indicates how strict the child sees his or her parents to be about smoking.

Experimental smoking

Table 24 shows the lifetables obtained for all the boys and all the girls separately taking the first report of any smoking as the terminal event.

The fourth column shows the proportion of those starting in 1974 as never smoked who survived as non-smokers in each year. To take account of the whole cohort these figures must be multiplied by the proportion who had not smoked before the study started i.e. 0.451 for the boys and 0.600 for the girls. To express the results in terms of the percentage uptake of smoking the adjusted figures must then be subtracted from one and multiplied by 100. The percentage uptake figures thus calculated are given in column five and plotted in Figure 12.

Table 24:

Life tables using the report of first smoking as the terminal event

Year	Number entering interval	Number of terminal events	Cumulative proportion surviving	Percentage uptake of smoking
Boys:				
1974	1392	0	1.0000	54.9
1975	1392	302	0.7665	64.4
1976	893	167	0.6141	72.3
1977	620	123	0.4828	78.2
1978	407	51	0.4174	81.2
1981	295	7	0.4064	81.7
1984	233	30	0.3492	84.3
Girls:				
1974	1935	0	1.0000	40.0
1975	1935	382	0.7868	52.8
1976	1267	241	0.6274	62.4
1977	871	139	0.5199	68.8
1978	612	78	0.4486	73.1
1981	447	15	0.4324	74.1
1984	369	38	0.3835	77.0

The cumulative proportion of children trying smoking by age and sex

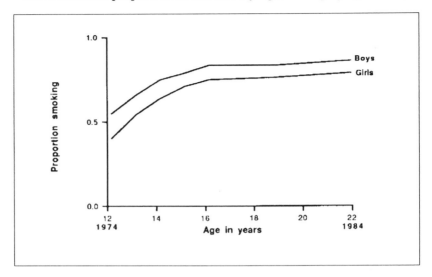

This shows how the proportion of children who had tried smoking increased between the ages of 11 and 21 for each sex. For a period of five years, from the first year of secondary schooling there were steady increases in the proportion of both boys and girls trying smoking. The rate of increase, which started at about 10% per year, diminished slightly each year to the end of the school period after which it became very slight. Consequently there was relatively little change in the proportion of children commencing smoking in the post school period.

The girls started with a lower proportion and since their trying smoking was at a rate only slightly higher than that of the boys the curves stay separated by an amount that slowly decreases from about 15% to 8%.

The equivalent lifetable calculations have been repeated for the children grouped according to the factors of interest, but only the resulting uptake curves are presented here. Figures 13 a) and b) show the patterns of uptake of smoking among boys and girls between the ages of 11 and 21, according to their awareness of the health hazards associated with smoking.

Figure 13:

The cumulative proportion of children trying smoking by age and according to whether they were dismissive or aware of the hazards of smoking (HAZ)

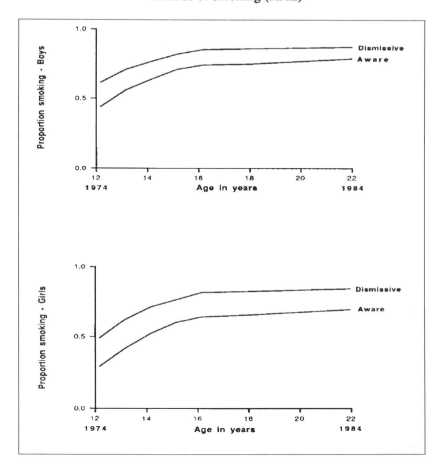

Boys and girls who had indicated at the onset of the study that only individuals who were old, who smoked "a lot" or who smoked over a period of many years were at risk from the health hazards of smoking were consistently more likely to have tried smoking. The incidence of trying smoking was slightly higher in this group so the curves diverged during the school period.

Figures 14 a) and b) show the uptake of smoking for both sexes according to their perception of peer pressure to smoke.

85

Figure 14:

The cumulative proportion of children trying smoking by age according to perceived peer pressure (PER)

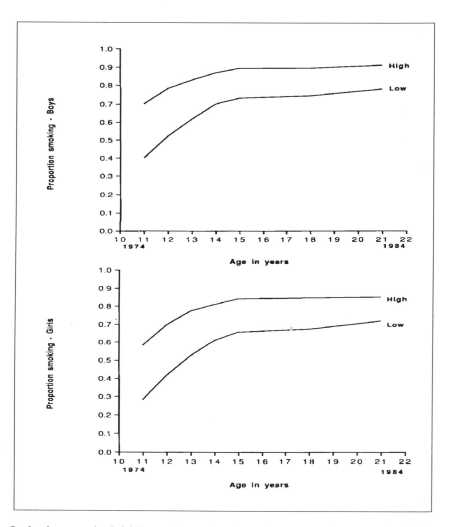

In both sexes the initial prevalence is substantially higher in those perceiving high peer pressure to smoke and the incidence throughout the period is very slightly higher in those initially perceiving peer pressure as low.

Figures 15 a) and b) show the uptake of smoking among boys and and girls between the ages of 11 and 21 according to parental smoking behaviour.

The cumulative proportion of children trying smoking by age according to parental smoking behaviour (PSM)

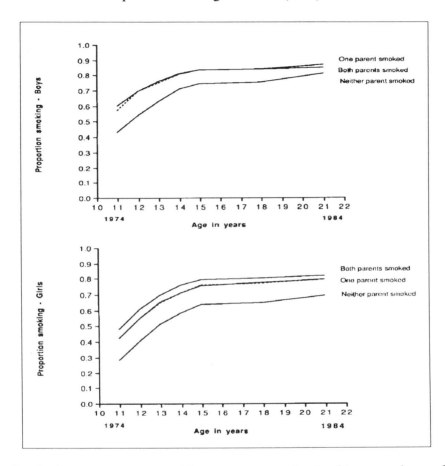

In the boys any parent smoking appears associated with a prevalence of 15-20% higher in 1974. The incidence of trying smoking is slightly higher in the group with no smoking parents so the curves converge slightly. In the girls the prevalence is markedly increased by one parent smoking and increased again if two parents smoke. The incidence appears relatively little affected by parental smoking and although the curves do converge it is only very slightly.

Figures 16 a) and b) show the uptake of smoking among boys and girls between the ages of 11 and 21 years according to their perception of parental concern regarding adolescent smoking.

Figure 16:

The cumulative proportion of children trying smoking by age and
parental concern (PCN), as perceived in 1974

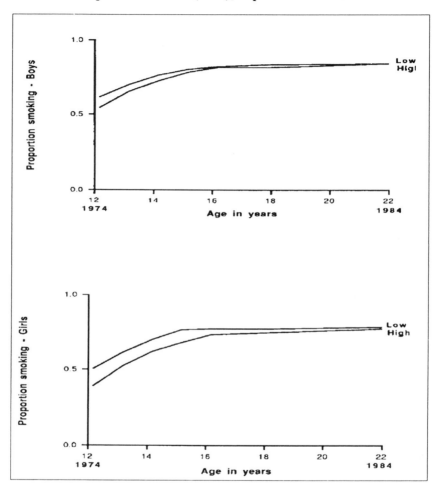

At the start of the study when the children were aged 11-12years the proportion
of both boys and of girls taking up smoking was lower where the child perceived
their parents as concerned about adolescent smoking. However, as the children
grew older the difference between the uptake of smoking in those who perceived
their parents as concerned about smoking and in those who failed to perceive
this, became progressively smaller, particularly among the boys.

The uptake of regular smoking

The life-tables giving the uptake of regular smoking for both sexes are given in Table 25

Table 25:

Life tables using the first report of regular smoking as the event

Year	Number entering interval	Number of terminal events	Cumulative proportion surviving	Percentage uptake of smoking
Boys:				
1974	2902	0	1.0000	6.0
1975	2902	138	0.9482	10.9
1976	2287	152	0.8801	17.3
1977	1797	353	0.6893	35.2
1978	1106	98	0.6227	41.5
1981	826	32	0.5945	44.1
1984	554	20	0.5710	46.3
Girls:				
1974	3144	0	1.0000	2.5
1975	3144	120	0.9584	6.6
1976	2504	176	0.8859	13.6
1977	1976	393	0.6952	32.2
1978	1282	134	0.6170	39.8
1981	965	44	0.5849	43.0
1984	686	13	0.5727	44.2

The uptake curves for "regular smoking" by both sexes over the study period are given in Figure 17.

Figure 17:
The cumulative proportion of children who have regularly smoked more than one cigarette per week by age

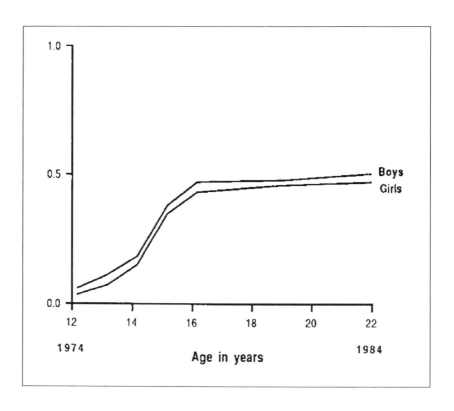

This plot shows a quite different pattern to that seen for experimental smoking. The incidences are low to start with, then in the middle of the school years there is a sharp increase in incidence which tails off in the last part of the school period and becomes very small after the school years. The proportion of boys taking up regular smoking still exceeds the proportion of girls, but the differences between the sexes are substantially less.

Figures 18 a) and b) show the equivalent changes in the uptake of regular smoking among boys and girls according to their awareness of the health hazards associated with smoking.

Figure 18:

The cumulative proportion of children who have smoked regularly by age according to whether they were dismissive or aware of the hazards of smoking (HAZ)

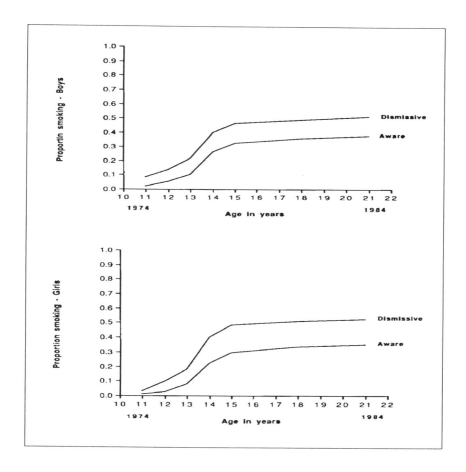

The differences between those who are dismissive of the hazards and those who are not follow the same pattern. There is an initial difference in prevalence among the boys which is not nearly so evident in the girls with the dismissive of both sexes having a slightly higher incidence.

The changes in the uptake of regular smoking for girls and boys between the ages of 11 and 21 years for those reporting themselves susceptible to peer pressure in 1974 are illustrated Figures 19 a) and b).

Figure 19:

The cumulative proportion of children who have smoked regularly according to their perception of peer pressure (PER)

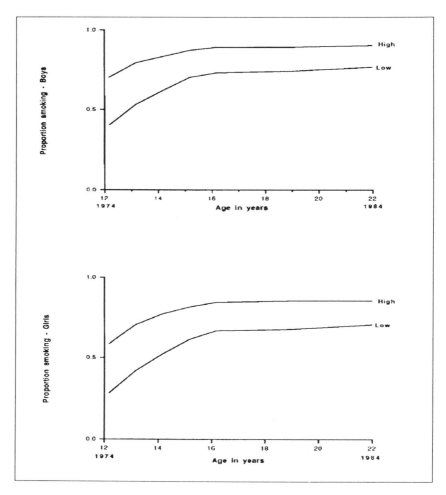

It is clear that children who initially reportwd themselves susceptible to peer pressure have a higher prevalence of regular smoking than their counterparts who were not susceptible. In addition the incidence appears to be slightly higher in those susceptible to peer pressure.

Figures 20 a) and b) show the uptake of regular smoking for both sexes within parental smoking groups over the study period.

The cumulative proportion of children who have smoked regularly by age according to parental smoking behaviour (PSM)

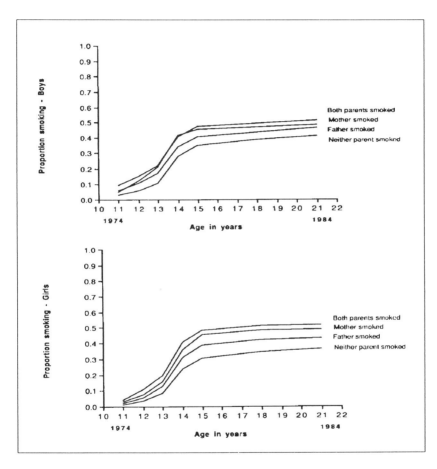

In both sexes there are initial differences in prevalence and a higher incidence in children with one or more smoking parent. In the boys there is evidence that the incidence is most high among those with the mother, but not the father smoking.

Figures 21 a) and b) show the uptake curves for regular smoking in both sexes according to whether they reported their parents as concerned about smoking or not.

The cumulative proportion of children who have smoked regularly by age and by parental concern (PCN) as perceived in 1974

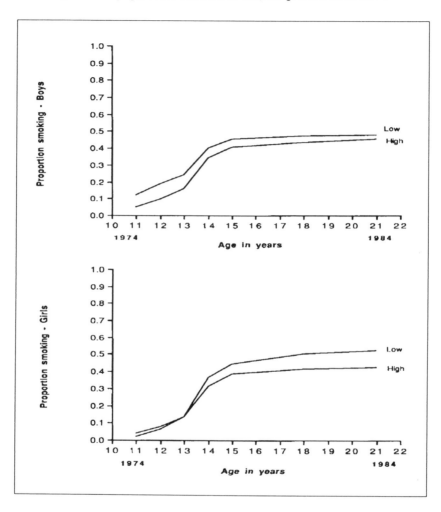

Initially there was quite a large difference in the boys, but the effect diminished slightly as they got older. Those who saw their parents as concerned started with a lower prevalence, but took it up slightly faster. The girls showed almost the opposite pattern. Those who saw their parents as concerned had only a slightly lower prevalence in 1974, but their incidence was consistently lower so the curves for the two groups diverged.

Summary

The results in this section show that the proportion of children who have tried smoking rises steadily to plateaus of 81% in the boys and 73% in the girls. Girls start with a considerably lower prevalence between 11- 12 years of age, but have a slightly higher incidence throughout.

The uptake of regular smoking increased, in both sexes, by less than 10% in the first two years and then increased sharply by 20% in the third year. There was a further increase of about 8% in 1978, the fifth year of secondary school. The prevalence then rose very slowly from then on to 1984 when the cohort was 21-22 years old. It appears that the really big increase in smoking is around the age of 14 years. It also appears that a child who reaches 16 years without smoking regularly is very unlikely to take up smoking subsequently.

The effects of the various factors, HAZ, PER, PSM and PCN, on the incidence of experimental smoking take the general form of what are sometimes quite large initial effects on the prevalences which then diminish because there is a higher incidence in the low prevalence groups. It appears that awareness of the hazards, peer pressure and parental concern, have had their effect on experimental smoking, good or bad, by the age of 11- 12 years and from that age on those previously deterred, by parental concern for example, appear to shake free and start to catch up with a higher incidence of experimenting.

Regular smoking, most obviously in the girls, seems to follow almost the converse pattern. The factors which have positive associations with prevalence, e.g. being dismissive of the hazards, are also in general positively associated with incidence which means that the uptake curves diverge. It appears that these factors only have temporary effects on experimental smoking, but more sustained effects on the uptake of regular smoking. This is evidence that altering the child's and the parents' attitudes or behaviour may well not have much effect on the incidence of experiments with cigarettes, but it may on the incidence of regular smoking.

4.7.2 Patterns over time

The complete pattern of a child's smoking history during the school period can be quite complicated. In each of the first three years a child could make any one of five responses. In the fourth and fifth year a sixth response:

'I used to smoke, but I have given it up'

was added to the questionnaire. This means that there were 5x5x5x6x6 = 4500 ways in which a child present in all five years might have responded. Some combinations are, in theory, not possible e.g. a smoking response followed by a 'never smoked' response, but this does not reduce the number of possibilities by very much.

There are two aims which analyses using the complete longitudinal data sets might have.

1. To identify and estimate the effects of factors associated with the uptake of smoking more reliably and precisely than in the earlier analyses;
    and
2. To identify particular patterns of uptake and associated factors.

The latter would be useful if subgroups susceptible at different times and to different potentiating factors could be identified. Such a situation would imply that combinations of several brief health education programmes with different content and timing might be more effective than one overall package at one time.

Both these issues can be addressed using appropriate analyses. The first aim can be approached by summarising each individual's pattern of uptake in some relatively simple way that uses all the data available from the 5 school years. By choosing a method that allows the use of children with incomplete data the number available for analysis is not so affected by the dropout rate.

4.7.2.1 Individual patterns of smoking uptake

There is no obviously correct way to summarise a sequence of smoking category codes. However the smoking categories can be considered to have a reasonably logical ordering. Because of this the average rate at which a child moves up the sequence of codes can be calculated and has a relatively straightforward interpretation.

The order of categories used was:

1. *Non-smoker*
2. *Tried once*
3. *Ex-smokers*
4. *Less than 1/week*
5. *Between 1 and 6/week*
6. *More than 6/week*

Regressing the codes, for those years when the child responded, on the year gave an average grade change per year. Because of the complex variety of patterns that occurred this figure gave a rather spurious impression of precision. For that reason the measure was simplified further by using it to classify each child into one of two categories. If the mean grade change per year was greater than 0.5 the child was classified as having increased their smoking rapidly. Table 26 gives the proportions of children classified in this way, as having rapidly increased their smoking, according to their 1974 characteristics.

Table 26:

Proportions of children who rapidly increased smoking between 1974 and 1978

1974 Factors	Category	Boys		Girls	
		N	% Smokers	N	% Smokers
Parental Smoking	1 Neither	888	23.0	985	27.6
behaviour(PSM)	2 Mother	395	28.9	448	33.9
	3 Father	670	27.9	676	33.4
	4 Both	908	30.0	908	35.9
Sibling smoking	1 No siblings	205	24.9	240	28.8
behaviour(SBS)	2 None smoking	1842	26.9	2006	29.8
	3 At least one smoker	814	30.1	771	40.1
Companions (COM)	1 No friends	394	27.2	573	22.9
	2 Friends of same sex	1963	25.4	1695	32.3
	3 Boy and girl friends	504	33.9	749	39.7
Organised Social	1 Not involved	1798	26.7	1747	29.0
activities (ACO)	2 Involved	1063	27.9	1270	37.0
Unorganised Social	1 Not involved	915	24.5	1206	27.8
Activities (ACD)	2 Involved	1946	28.4	1811	35.4

Table 26 contd...

Sports and games(SPG)	1 Not involved	692	27.3	1466	32.7
	2 Involved	2169	27.1	1551	32.0
Truants	1 Never	2752	26.9	2994	32.3
	2 Sometimes	109	33.0	23	39.1
Part-time job	1 None	2456	26.6	2759	27.6
	2 Has one	405	30.6	258	43.8
Perceived parental attitude to smoking (PCN)	1 Permissive	2438	28.4	2583	32.1
	2 Restrictive	423	19.9	434	33.6
General Parental Concern(PPM)	1 High	1663	26.7	1872	31.1
	2 Low	1198	27.8	1145	34.3
Sees positive reasons for smoking(FSM)	1 No	1869	25.9	2105	31.1
	2 Yes	992	29.5	912	35.2
Childrens beliefs about smoking (HAZ)	1 Realizes hazards	1048	24.4	1362	27.5
	2 Rejects hazards	1813	28.7	1655	36.3
Peer pressure to smoke(PER)	1 Low	1450	24.9	1815	30.3
	2 High	1411	29.5	1202	35.5
Attitude to school (ASC)	1 Satisfied	1364	24.9	1840	28.7
	2 Dissatisfied	1497	29.1	1177	38.1

From the changes with parental smoking it can be seen that the pattern of the relationships is similar to those seen for the 1978 prevalence of smoking. The table also shows that the girls, who generally have a lower prevalence of smoking, have rather higher proportions of 'rapid increasers'. This arises because on average the girls start smoking later than boys, but by 1978 they have almost caught up. They must therefore, on average, progress up through the smoking category codes more rapidly than the boys.

The same type of effect is seen in a comparison of the effects of parental attitude. The 1978 prevalence of regularly smoking more than 6 a week in those children who reported their parents as 'restrictive' (PCN; Appendix II) than it was in those whose parents appeared permissive. The prevalence were 19.7%

and 22.5% in the boys 16.1% and 21.1% in the girls. The differences are small and do not reach significance. However they are, if anything, in the direction one would expect if parental disapproval had some discouraging effect. The equivalent figures for the proportions of children in the 'rapidly increased' category are 28.4% and 19.9% for the boys and 32.1% and 33.6% for the girls. It appears that perceived parental disapproval does have some discouraging effect initially keeping those children in low smoking categories. However since they end up in 1978 smoking just as frequently they produce a higher proportion in the 'rapidly increasing' category. This effect appears in a number of other instances reducing and sometimes reversing differences in prevalences associated with the 1974 factors. Effectively the two approaches are showing the same thing with the second illustrating how the factor effects have diminished with time.

In the case of parental smoking the effect appears to persist as, on average, the parents' behaviour does not change much. In the case of perceived parental attitudes they either become less important to the child or the parents change as the child approaches adulthood. As a result the parental smoking groups differ in much the same way with respect to the prevalences as they do for the proportions classified as 'rapidly increasing' while the two measures show opposite effects when children who in 1974 saw their parents as 'restrictive' are compared with those who saw their parents as 'permissive'.

4.7.2.2 The relationship between patterns of development in smoking and attitudes

It is of considerable interest, from a health education point of view, to know whether children's attitudes change and for those that do whether this is before or after the child starts smoking. Consequently this section reports analyses aimed to make full use of the detailed longitudinal nature of the data.

For this analysis variables were created which uniquely identified all possible patterns of response over the five year period for smoking and a number of attitude questions asked throughout the school period of the study. The smoking responses over the five years were summarised with two variables. The first was designed to identify when if at all a child smoked his or her first cigarette in the period. The variable was constructed as a five digit number with a 1 for the years the child claimed never to have smoked and a 2 for the years he or she reported having either tried or smoked regularly. This meant that a child not reporting any smoking would generate the value 11111; a child reporting smoking for the first time in the fifth year would generate 11112. This process needs data for all 5 years so the analysis was restricted to those with data for every year. If a child was inconsistent, which occasionally happened, then the earlier report of smoking would be taken to be the correct one. That means that a sequence of 12122 would be treated as if it were 12222 in the analysis. A second such variable was designed to investigate the same relationships for really committed smoking behaviour of at least one per day, on average. This was constructed with the coding for each year as 2 for those regularly smoking >6 per week and 1 for the remainder. This was also used in the analyses to distinguish patterns of change associated with experimental smoking from those associated with the development of a regular smoking habit. Notice that this is not the same as the definition of 'regular' smoking used in earlier sections where it was used to indicate more than one per week.

The attitude sequences were also summarised with five digit variables using the responses to statements concerned with the hazards of smoking, the amount of peer pressure and the level of parental concern about smoking. For example the child's attitude to the hazards was represented for each year by the composite variable described in the earlier sections as HAZ (Appendix II). Thus if a child responded in any year with agree or strongly agree to any of the three statements that implied smoking was only a hazard if you were old, smoked a lot or had smoked for a long time then they were classed as 'dismissive' of the hazards. The five year variable was constructed with a digit for each year which was 2 if they were classed as dismissive and a 1 if they were not. Thus a child with the value 11122 had started by being aware of the hazards but had become dismissive by the fourth year 1976-7 and so on. Measures of peer pressure and parental concern described below were used in a similar way to construct variables describing how the childs perception of both had changed over the five years. Finally, the classification of children according to when they tried or took up regular smoking and when their attitude changed makes it possible to identify the sequence in which this happened. However, since questionnaires were only administered once a year there was quite a large proportion of children reporting changes of attitude and of smoking behaviour in the same year. In these cases the chronological sequence of events cannot be determined from the data. Nonetheless it is probable that one event did, precede the other in most cases. It is probably reasonable to assume that the indeterminate group divide into the different sequences in the same proportions observed in those for whom the sequence could be determined.

Smoking patterns

There were 1347 boys and 1560 girls with sufficient data for this part of the analysis. Of these 193 boys (14.3%) and 158 girls (10.1%) reported smoking and at some subsequent date denied it. These have been taken as positive from the first positive response. In some analyses only the unequivocal or decisive individuals have been used.

The patterns and the frequency with which they occurred for the incidence of first experimenting with smoking are given in Table 27

Table 27:

Distribution of children according to the year in
which they first reported trying a cigarette

		Boys	(%)	Girls	(%)
Decisive					
Never smoked	11111	291	21.6	444	28.5
First tried in					
1978	11112	48	3.6	77	4.9
1977	11122	75	5.6	104	6.7
1976	11222	79	5.9	164	10.5
1975	12222	128	9.5	186	11.9
1974 or earlier	22222	533	39.6	427	27.4
		1154	85.7	1402	89.9

101

Table 27 contd...

Indecisive
First tried in

1977	11121	20	1.5	9	0.6
1976	112--	30	2.2	22	1.4
1975	12---	35	2.6	39	2.5
1974	2----	7	8.0	88	5.6
		193	14.3	158	10.1

The equivalent figures for the children classified each year according to whether they smoked regularly i.e. >6 per week are given in Table 28.

Table 28:

Distribution of children according to the year in which they first reported smoking more than 1 a day

		Boys	*(%)*	*Girls*	*(%)*
Decisive					
Never smoked	11111	1083	80.4	1282	82.2
First tried in					
1978	11112	78	5.8	94	6.0
1977	11122	68	5.0	86	5.5
1976	11222	41	3.0	41	2.6
1975	12222	25	1.9	8	0.5
1974 or earlier	22222	6	0.4	3	0.2
		1301	96.6	1514	97.1
Indecisive					
First tried in					
1977	11121	14	1.0	21	1.3
1976	112--	18	1.3	14	0.9
1975	12---	7	0.5	8	0.5
1974	2----	7	0.5	3	0.2
		46	3.3	46	2.9

From these results it can be seen that 78.4% of boys and 71.5% of girls had tried smoking before they had completed their fifth year in secondary school. In fact 39.6% of boys and 27.4% of girls had tried before the age of 11 years. Regular smoking was much less likely and most children, 80.4% of the boys and

82.2% of the girls, completed the five years without at any time smoking more than 1 cigarette per day. However, smokers are less likely to produce a complete set of data for the five years than non-smokers and they are therefore under-represented in this group with data for all five years. In fact the prevalence of smoking in 1978 was 25.8% in the boys and 23.3 in the girls compared with 19.6% and 17.8% observed in this subgroup. This is because the proportion of those not smoking regularly in 1978 who produced a complete set of data for the five years was 47.1% while the equivalent proportion of those who were smoking regularly in 1978 who did was only 32.2%. This means that smokers were about one and a quarter times as likely to fail to respond at least once in the five years. The comparison of changes in smoking habits with changes in attitude internal to the sample are fortunately not very sensitive to such sources of bias.

Attitudes to hazards

The patterns describing the child's changing attitude to the hazards of smoking and their frequencies of occurrence are shown in Table 29. A code of 2 implies that the child was dismissive of the hazards. The opposite is described as 'aware' in that the child did not apppear to think the hazards could be ignored.

Table 29:
Distribution of children according to the year in which they first reported attitudes dismissive of the hazards of smoking

		Boys	(%)	Girls	(%)
Decisive					
Aware throughout	11111	183	(13.6)	319	(20.4)
Became dismissive in					
1978	11112	29	2.2	54	3.5
1977	11122	36	2.7	31	2.0
1976	11222	21	1.6	34	2.2
1975	12222	25	1.9	29	1.9
Total		111	8.2	148	9.5
Always dismissive	22222	197	14.6	142	9.1

103

Table 29 contd...

Became Aware in					
1978	22221	80	5.9	60	3.8
1977	22211	47	3.5	45	2.9
1976	22111	53	3.9	86	5.5
1975	21111	97	7.2	128	8.2
		277	20.6	319	20.4
Indecisive					
Initially aware					
1977	11121	46	3.4	62	4.0
1976	112--	73	5.4	84	5.4
1975	12---	125	9.3	145	9.3
Total		244	18.1	291	18.7
Initially dismissive					
	22212	47	3.5	33	2.1
	221--	90	6.7	82	5.3
	21---	198	14.7	226	14.5
Total		335	24.9	341	21.9

The majority of the children started by being 'dismissive' of the hazards i.e. 60.1% boys and 51.4% of girls. By 1978 the percentages were 41.6% of boys and 34.7% of the girls. Thus although the prevalence of smoking was rising during this period a decreasing proportion of the children were prepared to be dismissive of the hazards of smoking.

There were 13.6% of the boys and 20.4% of the girls who were 'aware' of the hazards throughout these five years of their secondary school education. On the other hand 14.6% of the boys and 9.1% of the girls were 'dismissive' of the hazards throughout the five years. This meant that just over a quarter of both sexes kept the same attitude throughout.

These were evenly split between 'aware' and dismissive in the case of the boys, but strongly favouring the 'aware' among the girls (20.4% aware, 9.1% dismissive). Of the children that changed their attitudes (71.8% of the boys and 70.5% of the girls) a proportion (about 30% of the total) changed decisively from one attitude to the other and a proportion (about 40% of the total) 'vacillated'. These in turn fell into two categories, those that started 'aware' and those that started 'dismissive'. Among the boys 8.2% started 'aware' and changed decisively to being dismissive; 20.6% started 'dismissive' and changed decisively to being 'aware'. This meant that of the 58.4% of the boys classed as 'aware' in 1978 there were 13.6% and 20.6% who had been decisive about it and the remaining 24.2% had changed their mind at least twice. Of the 65.3% of girls classed as 'aware' in 1978 there were 20.4% who had changed decisively to that view. This left 24.5% of the girls who had changed their minds at least twice. Finally there were only 26.3% of boys and 28.2% of girls who had changed from 'aware to 'dismissive' and only about a third of these had made up their minds decisively.

Experimental smoking and attitude changes

Attitudes to the hazards

The intention of this analysis is to determine in what sequence the child changed attitudes and tried smoking if, that is, he or she did either. Attitudes changed in both directions, but the change from 'aware' to 'dismissive' will be considered first. If a child started by being 'aware' and at some point became 'dismissive' and also, at some point reported smoking for the first time then one or other will have come first. Of course if they were reported in the same year the order cannot be determined from these data. Table 30 shows the boys according to the years in which they first reported smoking and were first classified as 'dismissive' of the hazards.

Table 30:

Boys classified by the year they first reported smoking in any form and the year they first showed a dismissive attitude to the 'hazards' of smoking

Year first reported smoking	Age (yrs)	*Year first classified as 'dismissive'*						
		1974 11-	1975 12-	1976 13-	1977 14-	1978 15-	After 1978	Total
1974		430	71	44	32	7	57	641
1975		98	22	14	6	3	20	163
1976		54	16	8	10	6	15	109
1977		58	11	6	6	3	11	95
1978		30	4	3	5	3	3	48
After 1978		139	26	19	23	7	77	291
Total		809	150	94	82	29	183	1347

105

Thus in 1974 there were 430 boys who reported smoking and were classified as 'dismissive' of the hazards. This and all the other frequencies on the diagonal represent boys who were first dismissive and first tried smoking in the same year. These give no information on which came first although they do indicate the proportion of boys in whom attitudes and behaviour change around the same time. There are 546 of these i.e. 40.5% of the total.

Those below the diagonal of the table reported changing attitude before reporting their first cigarette and there were 499 or 37.0% in this category. Above the diagonal were 302 of 22.4% of the children and these had reported smoking before indicating that they were dismissive of the hazards. Thus there were, 1.67 times as many of those with an identifiable chronology where the attitude had changed first. The difference was highly significant (McNemar's test $p \ll 0.01$). Thus, in 37.0% where the attitude had changed first, health education designed to maintain their awareness of the hazards during secondary school might well have a beneficial effect. The position may be even better than this. It could be argued that in all but those above the diagonal, health education programmes designed to increase awareness of hazards could be expected to have some effect. However, the 430 (31.9%) who were dismissive and had already tried smoking at the start of the study could obviously not benefit in this way from programmes after the age of 11 years. That leaves 615 or 45.7% who did not try smoking before secondary school and who started, or became, dismissive of the hazards before trying smoking. All of these children might benefit in this way from such health education between 11 and 12 years of age. In fact if all those 324 boys in this group who smoked were deterred it would mean decreasing the percentage of triers from 78.3% to 54.3% which is equivalent to deterring 30.7% of those who would otherwise have tried.

Table 31 shows the girls according to the years in which they first reported smoking and were first classified as "dismissive" of the hazard.

There were 575 (36.9%) girls in the diagonal cells of the table thus there were 985 (63.1%) in whom the relative timing of their changing attitudes and trying cigarettes could be determined. Of these 641 changed their attitude before they tried a cigarette, i.e. two thirds or 65.1% of those with an identifiable chronology. This is significantly more ($p \ll 0.01$) than the 50% to be expected if the two events are independent of each other and both of the orders in which the changes can occur are equally likely. This is strong evidence that the girls, even more than the boys, tend to have decided that the hazards of smoking do not really apply to them before they try their first cigarette.

There were 871 (55.8%) of girls who did not try smoking before secondary school and who started, or became, dismissive of the hazards before trying smoking. Of these 49.0% tried smoking during the five years they were at secondary school.

Table 31:

Girls classified by the year they first reported smoking in any form and the year they first showed a dismissive attitude to the 'hazards' of smoking

Year first reported smoking	Age (yrs)	Year first classified as 'dismissive'						Total
		1974 11-	1975 12-	1976 13-	1977 14-	1978 15-	After 1978	
1974		345	48	29	18	13	62	515
1975		125	34	21	8	7	30	225
1976		88	16	25	21	8	28	186
1977		41	14	8	14	7	29	113
1978		41	9	5	5	2	15	77
After 1978		162	53	30	27	17	155	444
		802	174	118	93	54	319	1560

The above exercise was repeated using the year the child first reported regularly smoking, more than 6 cigarettes a week, if they did. As might be expected this gave an even more definite picture. Over 80% of the children changed their attitude first. Only a very small proportion of children, less than 2%, actually reported smoking regularly whilst still apparently aware that the hazards applied to them. Of the 264 boys (19.6% of all boys) who reported smoking >1/day at any time only 20 (7.6% of the 264) had not already reported themselves as dismissive of the hazards. Among the girls 278 (17.8%) reported themselves as smoking more than 1 a day at least once during the five years. Of these only 31 (11.2% of the 278) were apparently still aware that the hazards were relevant to them. This indicates that over 90% of children who smoke regularly between the ages of 11 and 16 years become dismissive of the hazards before they smoke regularly.

Susceptibility to peer pressure with respect to smoking

This analysis required a full sequence of attitude responses covering the full five years. The three attitude questions concerned with peer pressure related to smoking used in the construction of the variable PER (Appendix II) discussed in earlier sections were not all included in the 1977 and 1978 questionnaires. For this reason a modified variable, based on the two attitude questions that were available for all five years, was constructed for this analysis. Children were categorised as susceptible to peer pressure in a particular year if they agreed or strongly agreed to either of the statements.

"Others make fun of you if you don't smoke"
"You have to smoke if you are with friends that are"

Of the 1254 boys with data for all five years, 384 (30.6%) appeared to be susceptible to peer pressure from the beginning while 516 (41.1%) were not classified as susceptible at anytime during the five year period. Among the 1483 girls 788 (53.1%) completed the five school years without at any time being classified as susceptible to peer pressure and only 346 (23.3%) appeared susceptible to peer pressure when they started secondary school in 1974. These figures mean that only 29.3% of the boys and 23.6% of the girls appeared to become susceptible to peer pressure during the five years.

Tables 32 and 33 give the distributions of the boys and girls respectively according to the years in which they were first classified as having tried smoking and first classified as susceptible.

Table 32:

Year first classified as susceptible to peer pressure
by year first tried smoking (boys)

Year first reported smoking	Age (yrs)	*Year first classified as susceptible*						
		1974 11-	1975 12-	1976 13-	1977 14-	1978 15-	>1978 16+	Total
1974		224	88	43	29	7	207	598
1975		45	24	5	7	5	58	144
1976		25	12	16	8	4	38	103
1977		24	7	8	8	4	42	93
1978		9	4	4	2	3	20	42
After 1978		57	21	26	12	7	151	274
Total		384	156	102	66	30	516	1254

Table 33:

Year first classified as susceptible to peer pressure by year first tried smoking (girls)

Year first reported smoking	Age (yrs)	Year first classified as susceptible						
		1974 11-	1975 12-	1976 13-	1977 14-	1978 15-	>1978 16+	Total
1974		155	66	17	19	6	24	487
1975		48	37	15	13	5	98	216
1976		40	15	14	12	2	87	170
1977		18	6	4	8	1	72	109
1978		18	5	5	4	2	40	74
After 1978		67	33	30	16	14	267	427
Total		346	162	85	72	30	788	1483

There were 565 (45.1%) boys above the diagonal who had clearly started smoking before being classified as susceptible to peer pressure. There were 426 (34.0%) on the diagonal for whom the order of events cannot be determined and there were 263 (21.0% below the diagonal who appeared to be susceptible to peer pressure prior to even trying a cigarette. Thus of those 828 boys for whom the chronology could be determined the vast majority (565 or 68.2% which was significantly more than 50%; p<<0.01) tried smoking before showing signs of being susceptible to peer pressure. The situation was similar among the girls. There were 1000 girls in whom the chronology of events could be determined and 677 (67.7%) smoked first.

Rather the opposite appeared to be the case for regular smoking. Table 34 and 35 give the equivalent results for boys and girls according to when they were first classified as susceptible and when they first reported smoking more than 6 cigarettes a week.

In 786 (62.7%) of the boys and 798 (53.8%) of the girls the sequence of events could be determined. In contrast to experimental smoking in only a small proportion of these (6.8% of boys and 8.0% of girls) did the change in smoking behaviour come before the change in attitude.

109

Table 34:

Year first classified as 'susceptible' to peer pressure
by year first reported regular smoking (boys)

Year first classified as susceptible

Year first reported regular smoking	Age (yrs)	1974 11-	1975 12-	1976 13-	1977 14-	1978 15-	>1978 16+	Total
74		6	1	1	1	0	4	13
75		12	6	2	2	0	7	29
76		24	20	4	2	2	15	57
77		23	12	5	6	2	23	71
78		30	11	5	1	2	23	72
After 78		289	116	85	54	24	444	1012
Total		384	156	102	66	30	516	1254

Table 35:

Year first classified as 'susceptible' to peer pressure
by year first reported regular smoking (girls)

Year first classified as susceptible

Year first reported regular smoking	Age (yrs)	1974 11-	1975 12-	1976 13-	1977 14-	1978 15-	>1978 16+	Total
74		1	0	0	1	0	4	6
75		5	1	0	1	0	7	14
76		16	10	1	4	1	20	52
77		28	21	6	3	2	41	101
78		26	13	5	6	1	38	89
After 78		270	117	73	57	26	678	1221
Total		346	162	85	72	30	788	1483

110

Perceived parental attitude to smoking

Each year the children were asked to indicate how much they agreed with the statement

"My parents don't allow me to smoke"

Using the responses from each year the children were classified according to the first year they perceived their parents as not actually disallowing them to smoke.

Table 36:

Distribution of boys according to the years in which they
first reported trying cigarettes and perceiving that their
parents might allow them to smoke

*Year the children first perceived their parents might allow
them to smoke*

Year first reported smoking	Age (yrs)	1974 11-	1975 12-	1976 13-	1977 14-	1978 15-	>1978 16+	Total
1974		127	76	65	73	35	156	532
1975		24	21	14	12	8	58	137
1976		17	9	7	6	4	44	87
1977		21	11	7	11	4	30	84
1978		2	10	2	3	4	16	37
>1978		35	27	26	28	5	104	225
Total		226	154	121	133	60	408	1102

Table 36 shows that 408 (37.0%) of the 1102 boys for whom these data were available were still reporting that their parents' did not allow them to smoke in 1978. There were 601 (54.5%) boys who had tried smoking while still believing that their parents would not allow it and only 227 (20.6%) who reported their parents allowing them to do so before they tried. Thus the great majority of boys who tried smoking did so while believing their parents would not allow it.

The girls data in Table 37 shows much the same pattern. Of the 1336 girls, 650 (14.9%) still reported that their parents did not allow them to smoke in the fifth year of secondary school. There were 599 (44.8%) girls who smoked while reporting that their parents did not allow it and 352 (26.4%) who only smoked after reporting that their parents did not disallow it. Again the majority tried before believing that their parents would allow it.

Distribution of girls according to year they first reported
trying cigarettes and perceiving that their parents might
allow them to smoke

Year the children first perceived their parents might
allow them to smoke.

Year first reported smoking	Age (yrs)	1974 11-	1975 12-	1976 13-	1977 14-	1978 15-	>1978 16+	Total
1974		134	50	45	27	26	161	443
1975		31	37	20	22	10	67	187
1976		37	15	19	17	4	70	162
1977		20	11	17	6	5	44	103
1978		4	11	9	9	2	31	66
>1978		63	45	36	43	1	187	378
Total		289	169	146	124	48	560	1336

The equivalent figures for regular smoking are given in Tables 38 and 39 and
from these a totally different pattern emerges.

Table 38:
Distribution of boys according to year they first reported
trying regular smoking and perceiving that their parents
might allow them to smoke

Year the children first perceived their parents might
allow them to smoke

Year first reported regular smoking	Age (yrs)	1974 11-	1975 12-	1976 13-	1977 14-	1978 15-	>1978 16+	Total
1974		6	3	1	1	1	0	12
1975		10	4	4	5	1	3	27
1976		13	6	9	7	8	7	50
1977		14	10	4	15	10	12	65
1978		17	7	5	5	13	13	60
> 1978		166	124	98	100	27	373	888
Total		226	154	121	133	60	408	1102

Table 39:

Distribution of girls according to year they first reported trying regular smoking and perceiving that their parents might allow them to smoke

Year first reported regular smoking	Age (yrs)	*Year the children first perceived their parents might allow them to smoke*						
		1974 11-	1975 12-	1976 13-	1977 14-	1978 15-	>1978 16+	Total
1974		1	1	0	0	1	2	5
1975		5	3	2	2	0	1	13
1976		13	7	7	4	3	10	13
1977		26	9	13	14	13	16	91
1978		22	9	7	11	13	14	76
>1978		222	140	117	93	18	517	1107
Total		198	169	146	124	48	560	1336

Only a small proportion of these children took up regular smoking during this period (19.4% of boys and 17.1% of girls) and therefore the overwhelming majority of the children perceived that their parents might allow them to smoke before they did so regularly (88.9% of the boys and 91.2% of the girls). However, these figures included a large number of children who may never smoke regularly (888 or 80.5% of the boys and 1107 or 82.9% of girls), but who nevertheless perceived that their parents had come to regard them as able to make adult decisions about smoking without them being authoritarian about it - 515 (58%) among the boys and 590 (53.2%) 9 among the girls. This may be uninformative in a health education sense. If we consider the children who did take up regular smoking i.e 214 boys and 229 girls then 75 (35.5%) and 69 (30.1%) respectively took up regular smoking while still perceiving that their parents did not allow them to smoke while 91 (42.5%) and 122 (53.3%) did not take it up until they perceived it to be permitted. Thus among those children that did smoke more than 6 per week rather more started to do so after perceiving their parents as allowing it than did so still thinking that their parents did not allow it. However, only in the girls was this difference significant (McNemar's test u=3.89; p<0.01).

113

4.7.3 Attributable fractions

A simple illustration of this method can be obtained by estimating the fraction of the boys regularly smoking (>1/ week) in 1978 attributable to the fact that they were dismissive of the hazards of smoking. There were 2050 for whom there was full information in 1978. Of these 496 (24%) were regular smokers and 1282 (63%) were dismissive of the hazards of smoking in 1974. There were 768 boys who were not dismissive of the hazards and of these 133 (17%) were regular smokers. Thus the proportion exposed P_{exp} = 0.63, the risk if not exposed is 0.17, and the risk if exposed is

$$(496 - 133) / (2050 - 768) = 363/1282 = 0.28$$

and the Odds Ratio is

$$(0.28 / (1-0.28)) / (0.17 / (1-0.17)) = 1.899$$

Using the formula for AF_p from the methods section the attributable fraction is,

$$AF_p = \frac{1282/2050 \ (363/1282 - 133/768)}{496/2050}$$

$$= 0.2842 \text{ or } 28.4\%$$

i.e. more than a quarter of the smoking in children appears to be attributable to their dismissive attitude to the hazards. This suggests that health education which maintained their awareness of the hazards might reduce the prevalence of regular smoking by more than a quarter.

However this is rather a simplistic approach and as discussed in the methods section it is generally necessary to take account of other factors which may cause biases in attributable fractions obtained from raw data. This is done by using logistic regression and the resulting estimates of odds ratios adjusted for the effects of other factors.

Being dismissive of the hazards is associated with a number of other factors which are in turn associated with an increased risk of smoking. Figure 7 gives the results from a logistic regression fit relating the boys 1978 smoking prevalences to the main 1974 factors. The calculations above using the raw figures simply compare the prevalences of the exposed and unexposed averaged over the various subgroups defined by the other factors. The model, on the other hand, identifies for individuals at each factor level how they differ, on average, from those in a reference base category with all factors at level 1. It provides an odds ratio for the 'exposed'.v.'unexposed' adjusted for the effects of other factors. The attributable fraction calculations require not only the odds ratio, but also the prevalence in the 'unexposed'. This means that it is necessary to specify which particular pair of 'exposed' and 'unexposed' categories are to be compared and to identify their make-up with respect to the other factors. Only then can the prevalence be deduced. Because the model is linear on the log-odds scale the coefficients represent how the 'exposed'/'not exposed' differ whatever the levels of other factors are as long as the latter are the same in each category. The constant term in the model, parameter 1 is the log-odds value equivalent to the prevalence for individuals with all factors at level 1. That is individuals of social class 1 with no parents smoking, no siblings, no companions, not involved in social activities, not susceptible to peer pressure to smoke and aware of the hazards of smoking. The fitted prevalence for this category is

$$p = 1/(1+\exp(+2.412)) = 0.0823$$

which is considerably lower than the 0.17 obtained for the 'unexposed' from the raw figures. Clearly for 'attributable fractions' to be interpretable it is necessary to define precisely the population to which they refer.

The group with all factors at level 1 except HAZ (the attitude to hazards factor) can be considered as a sample from a defined population. The prevalence of the 'unexposed' calculated above is 0.0823. That for the 'exposed' is obtained by adding the HAZ(2) coefficient to parameter 1 and transforming back i.e.

$$p_e = 1 / (1+\exp(-(-2.412+0.3773))) = 0.1156$$

Since the proportion 'exposed' i.e. who were dismissive of the hazards in 1974, is 0.63 the attributable fraction for this subgroup is

$$AF_p = \frac{0.63 \,(0.1156/0.0823 - 1)}{1+0.63 \,(0.1156/0.0823 - 1)} = 0.2031 = 20.3\%$$

This is smaller than the attributable fraction of 28.4% obtained from the raw data. This is partly because it refers to a different population with a lower prevalence, but adjusting the figures to allow for that still leaves it lower. The model fitting analysis shows that the magnitude of the effect seen in the raw data, from which the Odds Ratio is estimated as 1.899, is exaggerated. When other factors are taken into account the odds ratio, which is the anti-log (or exponential) of the logistic regression coefficient HAZ(2) is $\exp(0.3773) = 1.458$.

115

The attributable fraction obtained this way is free from bias, but it is not very informative for the population in general. It is better to use the more general approach described in the methods section to estimate the attributable fractions for the population represented by the whole sample. This is done by using the model to estimate what the prevalence would have been if none of the boys had been dismissive of the hazards, but all the other factors had remained the same. The prevalence estimated this way is 20.2% i.e a reduction of 24.2-20.2 = 4.0 which gives an attributable fraction of 4.0/24.2 = 16.5%. So once the levels of other factors are taken into account as well as their associations with the factor of interest the attributable fraction estimated for the whole population represented by this sample is reduced from 28.4% to 16.5%. To assess the part played in determining adult smoking by characteristics observed at age 11-12 years this method was used with the logistic regression analysis of the smoking at 21-22 years and the 1974 and 1984 risk factors. Using the logistic regression models relating the male and female prevalences of smoking in 1984 to the main 1974 and 1984 factors - Figures 10 and 11 - and modifying the data appropriately, fractions of the 1984 smoking attributable to the various factors can be obtained. These are given in Tables 40 and 41 for a number of the factors separately and in combination.

The models used included a range of factors representing the work situation (EMPS, SHFT, INJS, SC84) leisure activity (SPOR) and family smoking behaviour (PS84) in 1984. They also included factors representing attitudes (PER, HAZ), social activities (ACS, COM) and family background (SC74, PSM) as they were in 1974. Whether or not these factors may be manipulated by health education the fraction of smoking attributable to them puts an instructive perspective on their associations with the habit. Factors are included in the table if, for either the males or the females, the logistic regression coefficient is more than two standard errors from zero. This is equivalent to demanding that the approximate 95% CLs for the fitted odds ratio (the anti-log of the coefficient) do not include 1.

Table 40:

Attributable fractions of 21 year old smoking for 1974 and 1984 factors

Boys (n=1512; observed total prevalence 36.2%)

Risk factor level	Proportion of sample exposed	Risk factor level changed to	Predicted total prevalence(%)	Absolute reduction (r)	Attributable fraction(%) 100(r/36.2)
1984					
Unemployed	8.4	Employed	34.9	1.3	3.6
Shiftwork	23.7	No shifts	33.7	2.5	6.9
Low job satisfaction	70.6	High job satisfaction	34.7	1.5	4.1
No sport	38.4	Sport some nights	32.6	3.6	9.9
One or more parents who smoke	61.3	No parents smoking	32.4	3.8	10.5
1974					
Social companions	86.4	No companions	31.5	4.7	13.0
Social activities	42.4	No activities	32.9	3.3	9.1
Peer pressure	47.0	No pressure	31.0	5.2	14.4
Unaware of hazards	61.5	Aware	32.3	3.9	10.8
Combinations Peer pressure and/or unaware of hazards	74.9	No pressure and aware	27.3	8.9	24.6
as above and/or parents smoking	88.4	as above + parents not smoking	25.0	11.2	30.9
as above and/or no sport, low job satisfaction and currently unemployed	95.0	as above + some sport, employed and JS high	19.7	16.5	45.6

117

Attributable fractions of 21 year old smoking for 1974 and 1984 factors

Girls (n=1518; total prevalence 30.8%)

Risk factor level	Proportion of sample exposed	Risk factor level changed to	Predicted total prevalence(%)	Absolute reduction (r)	Attributable fraction(%) 100(r/30.8)
1984					
Unemployed	5.1	Employed	30.0	0.8	2.6
Shiftwork	15.6	No shifts	28.8	2.0	6.5
Low job satisfaction	71.4	High job satisfaction	29.2	1.6	5.2
No sport	56.8	Sport some nights	28.1	2.7	8.8
One or more parents who smoke	68.7	No parents smoking	27.1	3.7	12.0
1974					
Social companions	83.2	No companions	27.9	2.9	9.4
Social activities	40.9	No activities	28.0	2.8	9.1
Peer pressure	38.0	No pressure	29.5	1.3	4.2
Unaware of hazards	52.8	Aware	27.8	3.0	9.7
Combinations Peer pressure and/or unaware of hazards	65.1	No pressure and aware	26.5	4.3	14.0
as above and/or parents smoking	84.4	as above + parents not smoking	19.8	11.0	35.7
as above and/or no sport, low job satisfaction and currently unemployed	93.7	as above + some sport, employed and JS high	15.9	14.9	48.4

The table shows that 36.2% of these males smoke. The model showed that the 8.4% of males who were unemployed smoked more, on average. If they had been employed the model predicts that the total prevalence would have been reduced to 34.9%. This reduction of 1.3% expressed as a proportion of the observed total prevalence of 36.2% gives a figure of 3.6%. That is the fraction of the total prevalence due to increased smoking in the 8.4% unemployed. It is the fraction of smoking in 21 -22 year old males attributable to unemployment.

Thus although unemployment is significantly associated with increased smoking the increase is not sufficient, applied to only 8.4% of the sample, to account for very much of the smoking behaviour. Shiftwork is more common, 23.7% for males and 15.6% for females consequently the fractions attributable to it are 6.9% and 6.5% respectively, are larger although still small. Individuals involved in some sporting activity smoke less than those who do no sport. Taking 'no sport' as the risk factor the attributable fractions are 9.9% and 8.8% respectively. These figures are larger because the proportions 'exposed' to the risk factor, 70.6% and 56.8%, are much higher.

Parental smoking is also very common (61.3% and 68.7%) and a modest effect on smoking, i.e. a relative risk of about 1.5, translates into attributable fractions of 10.5% and 12.0% respectively.

The factors considered so far are from those operating contemporaneously with the smoking behaviour we are investigating. From the logistic regression we have seen that, in addition to these, factors identified 10 years earlier are independently associated with smoking in 21-22 year olds. In particular those boys who spent time with a social group of companions at age 11 years appear to be more at risk of eventually becoming smokers. Because this was true of more than 86.4% of the boys it appears as a large attributable fraction i.e. 13.0%. An equally large proportion of girls were in this category (83.2%), but it was not, in their case, associated with quite so much of an increase in their eventual smoking so their attributable fraction is smaller (9.4%). Early involvement in social activities follows much the same pattern in both sexes. The association with smoking is similar to that for 'companions', but the numbers at risk are less (42.4% for males and 40.9% for females) so that the attributable fractions are smaller, 9.1% and 9.1%. At the age of 11 years 47% of these boys and 38% of the girls reported peer pressure to smoke. This was significantly associated with increased smoking at 21-22 years for the boys and the attributable fraction was 14.4%. The factor did not appear to be associated with smoking in the girls to anything like the same degree. For the girls the attributable fraction was 4.2%. Rather larger proportions of the children appeared unaware of the true hazards of smoking (61.5% of the boys and 52.8% of girls) and the attributable fractions were 10.8% and 9.7% respectively.

The results discussed so far refer to each factor taken individually. However the factors cannot really be considered independently from one another in an assessment of what health education might achieve. Those who report peer pressure to smoke may well be, in some cases, the same individuals who appear to be unaware of the hazards of smoking. We need to take this into account when we estimate the potential effect of altering both these characteristics.

As it happens reported peer pressure and lack of awareness of the hazards do seem to be remarkably independent of one another. The individuals classified as either or both represent 74.9% and 65.1% of the boys and girls in the sample, but the attributable fractions due to these two factors are remarkably close to the sum of the two separate attributable fractions, 24.6% in the boys and 14.0% in the girls. This suggests an area where health education might have an impact. If the children's response to perceived peer pressure and knowledge of the hazards of smoking at 11 years could be altered and later smoking changed as the pattern of associations predict, then there is the potential of reducing smoking in young adults by up to nearly nearly one fifth. Considering children in this category plus those who have smoking parents, i.e. 88.4% boys and 84.4% girls, then the fractions of smoking attributable to this combination of risk factors are 30.9% and 35.7% respectively.

Finally, for completeness, if the risk category is extended to include those not involved in sport, with low job satisfaction and currently unemployed the attributable fractions of smoking due to all these risk factors operating in the population are estimated as 42.6% for males and 48.0% for females.

5 Discussion and conclusions

Study Structure and Analysis Strategy

At one time or another there were 8540 individuals in the study data set and at each stage a substantial sample from which to obtain very precise information on attitudes and behaviour. The longitudinal nature of the data, has made it possible to observe changes in both behaviour and attitudes as the children were followed for 10 years of their lives from the age of 11-12 year to 21-22 years.

As with all longitudinal studies there is a process of attrition arising from a gradual accumulation of non-responses. However, the analyses, which consist mainly of internal comparisons, are quite robust and not likely to be affected by the non-response. For certain analyses involving identifying the relative order of attitude and behaviour changes, the frequency of observation, at best once a year in the school period, was not sufficient for as precise an analysis as one would like. Nonetheless the analyses which were possible have allowed an unusual and interesting insight into the relationship between attitudes and behaviour.

The data structure makes possible analyses relating early factors to smoking behaviour at successively later stages. This shows how much of later behaviour can be predicted using these early characteristics and, in so far as the relationships identify causal mechanisms, indicate what form of health education programs might be most effective at deterring children from smoking. At each stage the respiratory health effects related to contemporaneous and earlier characteristics of the children have also been investigated. These analyses give some idea of the immediate health cost of the childs and their parents smoking behaviour which might add weight to health education exhortations.

Using the longitudinal nature of the data to identify when the children first reported particular smoking behaviour allowed the estimation of uptake curves. These have been used to compare the cumulative proportions of children who have succumbed at each age for various subgroups. They also indicate by the gradients of the plots at which ages the children are taking up the habit most rapidly. This has serious implication for health education programmes.

The comparisons of the sequences of attitude responses with those of smoking behaviour are necessary to resolve the problem of which changes first. If attitudes are largely developed to justify behaviours already adopted associations between them can hardly be taken as indicative of causal relationship which can be manipulated for health education purposes.

Finally the text reports the results of an analysis to assess the relative importance of the factors associated with young adult smoking. This had been done by estimating the fraction of the 21-22 year old smoking prevalence which can be attributed to various factors separately and in combination. These results make it possible to estimate the magnitudes of effects that health education programmes might have if they could alter the factors involved and thus modify later smoking behaviour by amounts proportional to the strengths of the associations.

Overview of Findings

Smoking

The factors associated with smoking behaviour have been investigated with regression analyses relating to 1974 characteristics, i.e. when the children were 11-12 years old, to smoking at 11-12 years, 15-16 years, 18-19 years, and 21-22 years. These showed that the important factors, with strong positive association, were parental and sibling smoking, spending spare time with opposite sex companions, being involved in social activities, peer pressure to smoke and being dismissive of the hazards of smoking. Once these factors were taken into account the fathers social class, parental concern about smoking and other parental attitudes and the children's own attitudes did not have significant associations.

The strength of the associations between 1974 factors and smoking diminished as the children became older, but persisted up to 1984 when the children reached 21-22 years. When 1984 characteristics involving employment and type of work were taken into account the association between smoking at that time and factors identified in 1974, ten years earlier, were not quite as pronounced as they had been earlier, but they remained clearly significant.

Uptake of smoking

The survival data analysis in section 4.7.1 shows that relatively few individuals, about 25%, go through school without trying smoking and that this is relatively independent of attitudes and circumstances. On the other hand a substantial proportion of individuals (~55%) avoid smoking regularly at any time before they reach 21-22 years and very few (~4.6%) take up regular smoking after 15-16 years. In addition the incidence of regular smoking during this period is associated with the attitudes and circumstances of the children which suggests that it might be modified. A very clear finding during this period is that the greatest incidence of both sexes is at about the age of 14 years. This has clear implication for the timing of health education programmes.

Chronology of attitude and behaviour changes

The findings of section 4.7.2 indicate quite strongly that attitudes to the hazards of smoking, peer pressure and opinions on parents' permissiveness do not have much influence on whether a child experiments with smoking. When such attitudes change in a direction favouring smoking, if they do, it is more often after the child has tried smoking. In the case of regular smoking the converse is true. The attitudes do tend to change in a direction favouring smoking more often before the child started to smoke regularly. These results confirm that for regular smoking, if not for experimental, that the chronological sequence of attitudinal and smoking behaviour development in the majority of cases is consistent with a causal relationship that might be modified by health education.

Attributable fractions of adult smoking prevalences

The attributable fraction investigation reported in section 4.7.3 (Tables 40 and 41) showed what fractions of the smoking in young adults could be attributed to various factors given the associations identified and the proportions exposed to the factors. There were effects due to a number of contemporaneous factors. That due to lack of involvement in active sport had the highest attributable fraction which was nearly 10%. Assuming a causal relationship this suggests that getting everyone involved in sport would reduce the prevalence of smoking by about a tenth. In this case such an assumption is unlikely to be justified, but it is helpful to illustrate the interpretation of attributable fractions. Parental smoking had an attributable fraction of 10.5% in the boys and 12.0% in the girls. However the most interesting finding is that factors identified when the children were 11-12 years old, in particular attitudes to peer pressure and to the hazards of smoking taken together had sizeable attributable fractions with respect to smoking 10 years later. Separately they were of the order of 10%, and in combination they were 24.6% for the boys and 14.0% for the girls. When parental smoking was also included with the two attitudes the overall attributable fractions became 30.9% and 35.7% respectively.

In conclusion the findings are essentially that:

   i) the fractions of smoking at 15-16 years and 21-22 years attributable to characteristics such as parental smoking and the child's attitudes to the hazards of smoking and peer pressure as they are at 11-12 years, are of the order of 30%.

   ii) the chance of an individual surviving to young adulthood without trying smoking is less than 30% and only a small number who reached 15-16 years without trying do so subsequently

   iii) the chance of an individual surviving to 21-22 years without at sometime smoking regularly (more than 1 per week) is about 55% and only a very few (~4.6%) take up regular smoking after 15-16 years.

   iv) the incidence of regular smoking of more than one per week is at its highest 20% between the ages of 13.5 and 14.5 years.

   v) the deterrent and provoking effects of factors such as parental concern and parental smoking appear to occur before 11-12 years of age as far as experimental smoking is concerned, but appear to have a continuing, though small effect, modifying the incidence, on regular smoking through out the school years.

and

   vi) attitudes to peer pressure, the hazards of smoking and parental concern appear on average to change, if they do change, in the direction of more tolerance to smoking after the children have experimented with smoking, but before they take up regular smoking.

These results indicate that there are several attitudes and circumstances, particularly susceptibility to peer pressure, a dismissive attitude to the hazards of smoking and smoking parents, at the age of 11-12 years which are significantly associated with later smoking. These associations are most clearly seen when the children were 15-16 years old, but they are still detectable, above and beyond the effects of contemporary factors, when the children have become young adults of 21-22 years of age.

The findings also indicate that there is not much chance of stopping a child experimenting since about 80% do so irrespective of attitudes and circumstances. However, they suggest that it may be possible to deter children from smoking regularly (more than 1 a week). No more than 45% do try smoking regularly and the results suggest that on average these children tend to change attitudes to the hazards of smoking, peer pressure and parental concern before doing so. In addition to this it seems that if children can be deterred from smoking regularly before the age 15-16 years they are relatively unlikely to do so subsequently. The results show that the maximum incidence of regular smoking occurs about the age of 14 years and the timing of health education programmes must take this into account.

This study has produced a lot of useful information in all the areas relevant to the design of health education programmes. However to assess its possible contribution it is necessary to identify precisely what the aim of such programmes should be. It might be possible to discourage children from experimenting during adolescence quite effectively by means that increased the likelihood that they would smoke as adults. In general such an approach would be considered ineffective. The main aim is to reduce the risk of the child becoming an adult smoker. However whether or not a programme has achieved that is extremely difficult to assess and most evaluations use the prevalence in the children as a yardstick for measuring success. Even this causes difficulties because the effects are small and prevalence generally proves an insensitive measure over the short periods available for evaluating progress in a research project. As a result it is common for such evaluations to assess effects using measures of understanding and knowledge that the programme was designed to increase. The increase in knowledge is assumed to decrease the risk of the child starting to smoke at school or later and thus decrease the risk that he or she would become an adult smoker (Reid; 1985)

Design of Anti-smoking Health Education Programmes

Obviously a good knowlege of the process, timing, environmental factors and attitudes associated with smoking uptake are necessary for designing an effective anti-smoking programme. However such studies as this needed to obtain that information take a very long time. In addition they can never be totally comprehensive and generalisable. As a result a good deal of health education has to be designed with current knowledge plus assumptions and refined by means of trial and error evaluations.

There are also subtle problems which arise because teachers, to some extent in contrast to health educators, see their role as providing knowledge and improving self-esteem and decision making skills rather than effecting behavioural change directly. (Reid;1985) This ties in with another problem raised by Kannas (1984), where he is critical of programmes requiring so much of the teachers or even special staff that they would be extremely difficult to implement in practice. He cites in particular Tell (1984) and Best (1983). He also draws attention to the difficulties of getting effective cooperation and thus implementation of the programme. This problem was encountered during the evelution studies of Murray, Rona et al (1984), Pederson (1981) and Lloyd et al (1983). It is clear that a useful programme must be designed so teachers are convinced that it is based on sound principles and are happy and able to incorporate it into their normal curriculum.

This study provides a considerable amount of unique information with which to reassess the nature, content and timing of health education programmes, but to do this it is necessary to consider the current situation. Reid (1983) presents a masterly overview of the current philosophy of health education programmes to reduce smoking in children.

He first summarises, from the existing literature, the reasons why children appear to take up smoking under the headings: Personal, Social and School factors. These findings have largely emerged from cross sectional studies, but the result of the longitudinal study reported in this text strongly confirms his identification of 'lack of real understanding of the hazards' as an important personal risk factor. The results here indicating the strong effects of peer pressures, sibling and parent smoking behaviour are also consistent with the findings he reports. However, Reid does not mention the immediate health effects of the children's own smoking nor the possible effects of passive smoking. These particular findings may prove useful in increasing the support and involvement of parents for health education programmes.

The effects of school factors have not been described in this text, but have been reported previously Murray, Kiryluk and Swan (1984) and are referred to in Reid's review. One possible development which would help reduce the smoking in adolescents would be a ban on teachers smoking. This may not yet be feasible, but health education programmes involving the teachers may have some effect on reducing their smoking behaviour and where possible this aspect of programme design should be maximised.

Reid concludes his review with a discussion of the need to gain the support of the schools in an area and to obtain their acceptances of a general policy on smoking in four parts:

1 *Defining and measuring goals*
2 *Curriculum development*
3 *Implementation of an agreed code of practice concerning smoking on the premises*
4 *Links with the community*

Assuming a school accepts the public health goal of reducing prevalence they will need first to establish baseline prevalences by a survey and then introduce approprate curriculum development.

Reid recommends a method known as the spiral curriculum involving four stages for different age ranges using different educational approaches available as HEC projects for the age ranges 10-12 years, 11-13 years, 13-16 years and 16-18 years. These are sensibly thought out and if well implemented should come close to maximising the possible beneficial effects.

However a number of authors reporting surveys or evaluations of health education programmes emphasise the preventive approach and thus the need to confront children at a very early age. These include O'Connell et al (1981), Calman (1985), Best (1983), Ledwith (1985) and Charlton (1986) although Charlton is reporting the first of a three stage program on the lines proposed by Reid. The results of the study reported in this text cast some doubts on the wisdom of this approach. They suggest that very early experimental smoking is not necessarily the same as the start of regular smoking. It appears that sooner or later a large proportion of children will experiment with smoking whatever the risk factors to which they are exposed and possibly whatever the health education they receive. Over the period of this longitudinal study it was the prevalence of regular smoking (one or more per week) which showed a tendency to be influenced by the various factors in the long term. Since the prevalences are low in the first year of secondary school (11-12 year olds), i.e. 6.0% of boys and 2.5% of girls, it is possible that studies and projects using younger children are analysing the prevalence of simple experimentation rather than of incipient regular smoking. This could mean that they are not producing very useful conclusions. It is not of course an argument against giving the children relevant knowledge at that age and assessing its retention. It is only a warning that assessment of the benefits by observing changes in smoking behaviour at this age may be quite misleading.

Reid's second stage refers to the 11-13 year age range. He points out that these are the years before the major increase in regular smoking occurs. This has been deduced largely from cross sectional studies. However, comparing the prevalence from two different groups of children a year apart in age is not a very reliable way of estimating incidence. The Dobbs and Marsh (1982) figures would suggest that the highest incidence for the boys was between the 3rd and 4th year when the prevalences were 8 and 20% (numerators of about 400). For the girls the highest 'incidence' appeared to be between the 4th and 5th years when the prevalence changed from 15 to 29%. Two years later the higher 'incidence' for the boys was between the 4th and 5th years and appeared to be 14% (31%-17%) while the girls in that year had their higher 'incidence' between the 3rd and 4th years 15% (24%-9%). Cross sectional prevalences from Wilcox and Gillies (1982) show a relatively steady rise in prevalence with no very obvious suggestion that there is a point where the incidence is greatest. The picture is, at least, ambiguous. However the results from this longitudinal study make it very clear that the boys and girls follow a very similar pattern of uptake, although the girls started with a lower prevalence, and the highest incidence, of about 18% in both sexes, occurs between the 3rd and 4th years. These data were obtained about 6 years earlier than the Dobbs and Marsh results in 1982, but they provide strong evidence that cross sectional studies are unreliable for estimating incidences. They also show that there is such a uniquely large incidence at a particular point in the children's school career that designers of health education programmes must identify when it occurs and take it carefully into account.

Finally the evidence from this study that susceptibility to peer pressure tends to develop before a child takes to smoking regularly suggests that health educationalists should make every effort to utilise the work of Evans (1981) concerned with equipping children to resist social pressures to smoke. The similar finding that children tend to become dismissive of the hazards before smoking regularly suggests that programmes should aim to create and maintain an awareness in the children of how relevant the hazards are to them.

In conclusion it is clear that although smoking in children is still a large problem the attributable fraction findings indicate that worthwhile effects can be achieved. The health evidence may make it possible to enrol parents in a much more constructive way than has been possible in the past. The relative chronology of changes in attitude and behaviour gives strong support to existing theories of health education and confirms the usefulness of elements already employed. Finally, there is strong evidence that a special effort, possibly involving new health education concepts, is needed at the point where the incidence of regular smoking is at its greatest.

References

1. Alexander HM, Callcott R, Dobson A J, Hardes G R, Lloyd DM, O'Connell D and Leeder SR (1983) Cigarette Smoking and Drug use in School children: IV - Factors associated with changes in smoking behaviour. Int J Epid 12,1, **p59-66**

2. Arkin RM, Roemhild HF, Johnson CA et al. (1981) The Minnesota Smoking Prevention Program. Journal of School Health Nov. **p 11-616**.

3. Baker, R.J. and Nelder, J.A. (1978) The GLIM system manual for release 3 Numerical Algorithms Group: Oxford

4. Best et al. (1983) The Waterloo Smoking Project, Proceedings of the 5th International Conference on Smoking and Health, Winnipeg, Canada.

5. Bewley B, Halil, T and Snaith AH (1973) 'Smoking by Primary School Children Prevalence and Associated Symptoms' Brit. J. Prev. Soc. Med. 27, **p150-153**.

6. Bothwell, PW (1959) 'The epidemiology of cigarette smoking in rural school children' Medical Officer, 102, **p 1225 - 132**

7. Bynner, JM (1969) 'The Young Smoker' Government Social Survey London HMSO

8. Calman ALH, Carmichael S, Deans HG, Calman KC (1985) Development of a primary school education programme with special emphasis on the prevention of cigarette smoking. Health Education Journal 2 **p65-69**

9. Charlton A (1986) Evaluation of a family linked smoking programme in primary schools. Health Education Journal 3, **p140-144**

10. Chave, SPW and Schilling, RSF (1959) 'The Smoking Habits of School children' Br J Prev Soc Med 13

11. Cox, D.R.(1972) Regression models and life tables (with discussion) J.R.Statist. Soc.B,34,**187-202**

12. Deans G, Calman A, Carmichael S. (1984) Smoking interventions in the primary school - some implications of an evaluation of a recently developed programme. Paper presented at 2nd National Conference on Health Education and Youth, University of Southampton.

13. Dobbs, J and Marsh, A (1983) 'Smoking among secondary school children' OPCS Survey London HM S O

14. Doll R (1984) Smoking and Death Rates J. of the Am. Med Ass. 251 (21) **p 2854 - 2857**, June 1

15. Doll R and Hill AB (1964) 'Mortality in Relation to Smoking: 10 years observation of British Doctors' BMJ 1 **1399-1460**

16. Dyke, G.V. and Patterson, H.D. (1952) Analysis of factorial arrangements when the data are proportions. Biometrics, 8, **1-12**

17. Evans RI, et al. (1981) Social modelling films to deter smoking in adolescents: results of a three year field investigation. J. of Applied Psychology, 66: **399-414**.

18. Fisher DA, Armstrong DK, de Klerk NH. (1983) A randomised controled trial of education for prevention of smoking in 12 year-old children. Proceedings of the 5th World Congress on Smoking and Health, Winnipeg, Canada, July

19. Flay B R, Hansen W B, Johnson C A, Sobel J L. (1983) Involvement of children in motivating parents to quit smoking with a television programme. (Health Behaviour Research Institute, University of Southern California.) Paper presented at the 5th World Conference on Smoking and Health, Winnipeg, Canada.

20. Gillies PA, Elwood JM, Pearson JCG and Cust G (1987) 'An adolescent smoking survey in Trent and its contribution to health promotion.' Health Education J 46, 1, **p 19-22**

21. The GLIM System Manual Release 3.77 (1985) Numerical Algorithms Group, Oxford

22. Greenberg JS, Deputat Z. (1978) Smoking intervention: Comparing three methods in a high school setting. J School Health. Oct. **p 498-502**

23. Hammond and Horn (1958) Smoking and death rates - report on forty-four months of follow-up of 187,783 men. J. of Am. Med Ass 166: **1294-1308** Mar 15.

24. Hardes GR, Alexander HM, Dobson AJ, Lloyd DM, O'Connell D, Purcell I and Leeder S R (1981) Cigarette smoking and drug use in School children in the Hunter region (NSW) I - Tobacco, Alcohol and Analgesic use in 10-12 year old primary school children (1979)
Med J Aust 1:**p579-581**

25. Holland, W W and Elliott A (1968), Cigarette smoking, respiratory symptoms and anti-smoking propaganda Lancet, 1 **p 41-43**

26. Jefferys M, Norman-Taylor W and Griffiths, G (1967) Long term results of an anti-smoking educational campaign. Medical Officer 117, **p 93-95**

27. Kannas L. (1984) Role and development of prevention programs of smoking in schools. Paper presented at Symposium on Smoking and Health in the South European countries, Barcelona.

28. Kannas L (1985) The Image of the Smoking and the Non-smoking Young Person Health Education J 44, 1, **p26-30**

29. Kendall M G and Stuart A (1961) The Advanced Theory of Statistics: Vol 2 Griffin, London.

30. Ledwith F. (1985) The evaluation of a secondary school smoking education intervention. Dept of Education, University of Manchester. Report to the Scottish Health Education Group.

31. Lloyd DM, Alexander HM, Callcott R, Dobson AJ, Hardes GR, O'Connell D, and Leeder SR (1983) Cigarette smoking and drug use in Schoolchildren III - Evaluation of a smoking prevention education programme. Int J Epid 12,1, **p51-58 32.** London Borough of Merton (1986) The Reorganisation of Education' Crown House, London Rd., Morden, Surrey.

33. Luepker RV. Johnson CA, Murray DM, Pechacek TF.(1983) Prevention of cigarette smoking: three year follow-up of an education program for youth. Journal of Behavioural Medicine, 6: **53-62**.

34. McGuffin S.(1982) Smoking - the knowledge and behaviour of children in N. Ireland. Health Education Journal, 41: **53-59**.

35. Milne, A., Marshall-Mies, J and Coleman JC (1975) 'A study of the impact of the Schools Health Curriculum Project on Knowledge Attitudes and Behaviour of Teenage Students' Education and Public Affairs Washington

36. Murray M, Kiryluk S, Swan AV (1984) School Characteristics and Adolescent Smoking. Results from the MRC/Derbyshire Smoking Study 1974-8 and from a follow-up in 1981 J. Epid Comm Health 38 , **p 167-172**

37. Murray M, Swan AV, Clark G.(1984) Long term effect of a school-based anti-smoking programme. J. Epidem. Comm. Health 38: **p247-252**.

38. Murray M, Swan AV, Enock G, Johnson MRD, Banks MH, Reid DJ (1982) The effectiveness of the Health education Councils' 'My Body' School education project. Health Educ. J. 41, **p. 126-130**.

39. Murray M, Rona RJ, Morris RW, Tait N.(1984) The smoking and dietary behaviour of Lambeth school children. I. The effectiveness of an anti-smoking and nutrition education programme for children. Public Health, London 98: **163-172**.

40. Nelder, JA and Wedderburn, RWM (1972) Generalised linear models J.R.Statist.Soc.A, 135,**370-384**.

41. Nelson SC, Budd RJ, Eiser JR, Morgan M, Gammage P, Gray E.(1985) The Avon prevalence study: A survey of cigarette smoking in secondary school children. Health Educational Journal; 44, 1, **p12-15**

42. Newman IM. (1984) Pressures affecting teenage smoking. In G Campbell(ed) Health education and Youth: a review of research and development. London: Falmer Press.

43. Newman B.(1983) Why do young children smoke? Proceedings of the 5th World Conference on Smoking and Health. Winnipeg, Canada.

44. O'Connell D, Alexandra HM, Dobson AJ, Lloyd DM, Hardes GR, Springthorpe HJ and Leeder S R (1981) Cigarette Smoking and Drug use in School children II Factors associated with Smoking Int J Epid 10,3, **p223-231**

45. O'Rourke, A and Wilson-Davis, K (1970) 'Smoking and schoolchildren' J Roy Coll. Gen Practit 20 **p354 - 360**

46. OPCS (1977) General Household Survey 1974 London: HMSO

47. OPCS (1978) 1970-1972 Ocupational Mortality London: HMSO

48. Pederson LL, Baskerville Jon C, Lefcoe NW.(1981) Change in smoking status among school-aged youth: impact of a smoking awareness curriculum. American Journal of Public Health, 71: **p1401-04**.

49. Perry CL, Telch MJ, Killen J et al.(1983) High school smoking prevention: The relative efficacy of varied treatments and instructors. Adolescence, 71: **561-566**.

50. Reid, D.J. (1985) 'Prevention of smoking among school children: recommendations for policy development' Health Educ. J 44, **p3-12**

51. Roethlisberger FJ and Dickson WJ (1939) Management and the Worker Harvard University Press, Cambridge, Massachusetts US.

52. Royal College of Physicians (1962) Smoking and Health Pitman's Medical, London.

53. Schinke SP, Lewayne D, Gilchrist LD, Snow WH (1985) Skills intervention to Prevent Cigarette Smoking among Adolescents. Am J Pub Health 75, 6, **p665-667**

54. Swan, AV (1985) 'Fitting Linear Models by Maximum Likelihood Methods to Grouped and Ungrouped Binomial Data'. GLIM Newsletter 11, **pp. 16-17.**

55. Tell GS, Klepp KI, Vellar OD, McAlister A.(1984) Preventing the onset of cigarette smoking in Norwegian adolescents: The Oslo youth study. Preventive Medicine. 13: **256-275.**

56. Thompson EL. (1978) 'Smoking Education Programmes 1960-1976' Am   J Pub Health 68 (3), **p 250-257**

57. US Surgeon General (1979) Smoking and Health. US Department of Health, Education and Welfare Public Health Service. Washington 1979

58. Watson, LM (1966) Cigarette smoking in schoolchildren: A study of the effectiveness of different health education methods in modifying behaviour knowledge and attitudes, Health Bulletin, 24 (1) **p 5-12**

59. Wilcox, B., Engel, E., Reid, D.J   (1978) 'Smoking Education in Children: UK trials of an international project'. Int J Health   Educ XXI **p236-244**

60. Wilcox B, and   Gillies PA (1982) 'Smoking education in Sheffield secondary schools 1980-82' Report to the Health Education Council

61. Wilcox B and Gillies PA (1984) Prevalence of Smoking among school children in Sheffield - Planning for   Prevention. Health Education J 43, 2&3, **p57-59**

APPENDIX I
QUESTIONNAIRES USED

CONFIDENTIAL

c.c. 1 2 3 4 5 6 7 8 9 10 11

EACH CARD | H | S | P | C | 7 | 4 | 08303 |

MRC/DERBYSHIRE SMOKING STUDY
SCHOOLCHILD QUESTIONNAIRE (1ST YEAR)

Your answers to these questions will help us to find out more about smoking and how it affects the health of young people. Please answer all the questions. All your replies will be strictly confidential. Your parents and teachers will not see them. They will be seen only by the medical research team.

When you have answered all the questions, please put this questionnaire in the envelope and seal it.

Now turn over the page and begin.

139

PLEASE WRITE IN BLOCK CAPITALS

YOUR LAST NAME _____

YOUR FIRST NAME(S) _____

WHAT IS YOUR DATE OF BIRTH? Please write this in numbers. For example 1st June 1962 would be:-

0 1	0 6	19 6 2
Date	Month	Year

A guide to the number of each month is given for you:-

JAN	FEB	MAR	APR	MAY	JUNE	JULY	AUG	SEPT	OCT	NOV	DEC
0 1	0 2	0 3	0 4	0 5	0 6	0 7	0 8	0 9	1 0	1 1	1 2

NOW WRITE YOUR OWN DATE OF BIRTH IN THESE BOXES.

		19
Date	Month	Year

WHAT SEX ARE YOU? (Please tick one box)

BOY ☐ 1   GIRL ☐ 2

WRITE THE FULL NAME OF YOUR SCHOOL _____

SCHOOL NUMBER (your teacher will tell you this)

☐☐☐☐

WHAT FORM ARE YOU IN? _____

These first questions concern your health. Please make sure that you answer every question, whether you smoke or not.

1) Do you usually cough first thing in the morning?
(please tick one box)

YES ☐ 1

NO ☐ 2

2) Do you cough during the day or at night?
(Please tick one box)

YES ☐ 1

NO ☐ 2

3) Do you get short of breath when hurrying on flat ground or walking up a slight hill?
(please tick one box)

YES ☐ 1

NO ☐ 2

4) Please read these statements carefully and tick the one box which best describes you. (tick one box only)

I have never smoked a cigarette. ☐ 1

I have only ever tried smoking once. ☐ 2

I have smoked sometimes, but I don't smoke as much as one a week. ☐ 3

I usually smoke between one and six cigarettes a week. ☐ 4

I usually smoke more than six cigarettes a week. ☐ 5

5) Since this time last week how many cigarettes have you smoked?

(Write the figure in the box; if you haven't smoked any, write 0.) ☐

6) I smoke with OTHER PEOPLE ....
   (tick one box only)

   ..... most of the time   ☐ 1

   ..... sometimes   ☐ 2

   ..... hardly ever   ☐ 3

   I don't smoke   ☐ 4

7) I smoke BY MYSELF ....
   (tick one box only)

   ..... most of the time   ☐ 1

   ..... sometimes   ☐ 2

   ..... hardly ever   ☐ 3

   I don't smoke   ☐ 4

8) If you have EVER smoked a cigarette, we would like you to tell us why you did so.

If you have NEVER smoked, tick this box.

I HAVE NEVER SMOKED ☐ 1

If you have smoked, please tick one box on each line below.
I smoked because ....

		YES	NO
.... my mother or father smokes		☐ 1	☐ 2
.... my friends smoke		☐ 1	☐ 2
.... I wanted to feel grown-up		☐ 1	☐ 2
.... my brother or sister smokes		☐ 1	☐ 2
.... I was dared to smoke		☐ 1	☐ 2

Please write in any other reason _____

_____

9) Does your father smoke cigarettes?
(please tick one box)

Yes ☐ 1

No ☐ 2

I don't know ☐ 3

I have no father ☐ 4

10) Does your father smoke a pipe or cigars?
(please tick one box)

Yes ☐ 1

No ☐ 2

I don't know ☐ 3

I have no father ☐ 4

143

11) Does your mother smoke cigarettes?
(please tick one box)

Yes [ ] 1

No [ ] 2

I don't know [ ] 3

I have no mother [ ] 4

12) How many brothers do you have? [ ]

How many of them smoke cigarettes?
(Put figures in the boxes.) [ ]

13) How many sisters do you have? [ ]

How many of them smoke cigarettes?
(Put figures in the boxes.) [ ]

14) How many of your friends IN THIS SCHOOL smoke cigarettes?
(please tick one box)

All of them [ ] 1

Most of them [ ] 2

Half of them [ ] 3

A few of them [ ] 4

None [ ] 5

144

15) How many of your friends WHO DON'T COME TO THIS SCHOOL smoke cigarettes?
(please tick one box)

All of them	☐ 1
Most of them	☐ 2
Half of them	☐ 3
A few of them	☐ 4
None	☐ 5

16) How many evenings a week do you USUALLY spend doing homework?
(please tick one box.)

5 or more evenings a week	☐ 1
3 or 4 evenings	☐ 2
1 or 2 evenings	☐ 3
No evenings	☐ 4

17) How many evenings a week do you USUALLY go out?
(please tick one box.)

5 or more evenings	☐ 1
3 or 4 evenings	☐ 2
1 or 2 evenings	☐ 3
No evenings	☐ 4

18) What kind of things do you do in your spare time?
   (Tick as many boxes as you like.)

   Sports and games   ☐ 1

   Go to the cinema   ☐ 1

   Scouts or Boys Brigade   ☐ 1

   Guides or Girls Brigade   ☐ 1

   Music or a hobby, e.g. fishing, horseback riding   ☐ 1

   Go dancing   ☐ 1

   Go around with a group of my own age   ☐ 1

   Watch T.V. or play records   ☐ 1

   Mess around   ☐ 1

   Go to a youth club   ☐ 1

   Read   ☐ 1

   Help out at home, in the house or on a farm.   ☐ 1

   Anything else _____
   (please describe)

---

19) With whom do you spend MOST of your spare time?
   (please tick one or more boxes)

   A group of boys   ☐ 1

   A group of girls   ☐ 1

   A boyfriend or girlfriend   ☐ 1

   A friend   ☐ 1

   A group of boys and girls   ☐ 1

   My parents   ☐ 1

   On my own   ☐ 1

   I don't go out much   ☐ 1

   Anything else _____
   (please describe)

20) Do you have a part-time job outside school hours?
(please tick one box)

Yes ☐ 1   No ☐ 2

If YES, what kind of job is this? _____
_____

21) How much money PER WEEK do you spend on yourself?
(put the amount in figures)

£ ☐☐ p

2) How much money PER WEEK do you save?

£ ☐☐ p

23) Out of lesson time, what school teams, clubs or societies do you belong to?

Sports or games teams (e.g., football, hockey etc)   ☐ 1

Music or drama   ☐ 1

Art or handicraft   ☐ 1

None   ☐ 1

Anything else _____
_____

24) Have you played truant or skived from school?
(please tick one box)

Never   ☐ 1

Once or twice   ☐ 2

Sometimes   ☐ 3

Often   ☐ 4

28) Here are some statements, opinions and ideas about smoking and school life. We would like you to tell us whether you agree with them. If you agree with a statement, put a tick by it in the column marked "agree." If you disagree, please tick the column marked "disagree." If you agree very much, tick the column marked "strongly agree." If you disagree very much, tick the column marked "strongly disagree." If you really don't know whether you agree or disagree, tick the column marked "dont know."

Put one tick in each row.

For example, 'Derby County is a good football team'. If you very much agree with this, you will tick the "strongly agree" column, like this:

	Strongly Agree	Agree	Don't Know	Disagree	Strongly Disagree
Derby County is a good football team.	✓	☐	☐	☐	☐

Now do the same for each of the statements. Please read each one carefully before you answer. Remember one tick for each statement.

	Strongly Agree	Agree	Don't Know	Disagree	Strongly Disagree
1 Smoking can help people when they feel nervous or embarassed.	☐ 1	☐ 2	☐ 3	☐ 4	☐ 5
2 Most of my friends smoke cigarettes.	☐ 1	☐ 2	☐ 3	☐ 4	☐ 5
3 My parents are stricter than my teachers about smoking.	☐ 1	☐ 2	☐ 3	☐ 4	☐ 5
4 I am fed up with school.	☐ 1	☐ 2	☐ 3	☐ 4	☐ 5
5. My parents are upset if I do badly in my schoolwork.	☐ 1	☐ 2	☐ 3	☐ 4	☐ 5
6 Smoking is very enjoyable.	☐ 1	☐ 2	☐ 3	☐ 4	☐ 5
7 Smoking is dangerous only to older people.	☐ 1	☐ 2	☐ 3	☐ 4	☐ 5

		Strongly Agree	Agree	Don't Know	Disagree	Strongly Disagree
8.	A pupil who plays truant or skives from school should be punished.	1	2	3	4	5
9.	Cigarettes should be harder to get.	1	2	3	4	5
10	Others make fun of you if you don't smoke.	1	2	3	4	5
11.	Sometimes my brother or sister gives me a cigarette.	1	2	3	4	5
12.	My parents do not mind whom I go around with.	1	2	3	4	5
13	Smoking is a dirty habit.	1	2	3	4	5
14	Smoking is only bad for you if you smoke a lot.	1	2	3	4	5
15.	It is all right to tell a lie to a teacher to get out of trouble.	1	2	3	4	5
16.	You have to smoke when you're with friends who smoke.	1	2	3	4	5
17.	My parents don't allow me to smoke.	1	2	3	4	5
18.	My parents would like me to have a better job than my father's when I leave school.	1	2	3	4	5
19.	There is nothing wrong with copying from someone else in a school test.	1	2	3	4	5
20	I would do what my friends want rather than what my parents want.	1	2	3	4	5
21	Sometimes one of my parents gives me a cigarette.	1	2	3	4	5

		Strongly Agree	Agree	Don't Know	Disagree	Strongly Disagree
22.	I like boys and girls who fool around in class.	☐ 1	☐ 2	☐ 3	☐ 4	☐ 5
23	Children caught smoking should be punished.	☐ 1	☐ 2	☐ 3	☐ 4	☐ 5
24	Smoking is only bad for you if you have been smoking for many years.	☐ 1	☐ 2	☐ 3	☐ 4	☐ 5
25.	Pupils who look untidy in school should be told off.	☐ 1	☐ 2	☐ 3	☐ 4	☐ 5
26	There is nothing wrong with smoking.	☐ 1	☐ 2	☐ 3	☐ 4	☐ 5
27.	Pupils should not be cheeky to the teacher.	☐ 1	☐ 2	☐ 3	☐ 4	☐ 5

This is the end of the questions. Now check to see that you have answered all the questions, and if you have any comments on the questionnaire write them in the space below.

Thank you very much.

150

CONFIDENTIAL

cc. 1 2 3 4 5 6 7 8 9 10 11 12 13 14 15 16

| H | S | P | T | 7 | 5 | 0 0 0 1 5 | 1 | | |

MRC/DERBYSHIRE SMOKING STUDY
TEACHERS' QUESTIONNAIRE

Dear Teacher,

The Derbyshire Health and Education Committees are co-operating with St. Thomas's Hospital, London, in an enquiry into smoking, health and related factors in a population of secondary school children. This study is taking place over a five year period. One of the aims of the study is to find effective anti-smoking techniques.

A number of studies have already shown that there are differences in the amount of smoking between types of schools. This research is endeavouring to identify factors that may be important within schools.

We would be very grateful if you could complete this anonymous questionnaire, whether you smoke or not.

We hope you will feel able to assist us with this very important study. Your answers will, of course, be treated in strict confidence by the medical research team.

Yours sincerely,

Dr. P.K. Sylvester,
Area Medical Officer,
Derbyshire Area Health Authority

Mr. C. W. Phillips,
Director of Education.

Prof. W. W. Holland,
Professor of Clinical Epidemiology
& Social Medicine,
St. Thomas' Hospital,
London SE1 7EH.

151

The first few questions are concerned with several personal details.

---

1. In what year were you born?

    19 [|]

---

2. Sex: (please tick the appropriate box)

    Male   [ ] 1

    Female [ ] 2

---

3. How long have you been teaching at this school?

    [|]   [|]
    Years   Months

---

4. a) Do you teach full-time or part-time at this school?

    Full - time   [ ] 1

    Part - time   [ ] 2

    b) *If part-time,* how many hours per week do you spend teaching at this school?

    Less than 5 hours   [ ] 1

    5 – 10 hours   [ ] 2

    11 – 15 hours   [ ] 3

    16 – 20 hours   [ ] 4

    More than 20 hours [ ] 5

152

The next questions concern your own smoking habits, if any.

5. Have you ever smoked cigarettes? (i.e., at least 1 cigarette per day or 1 oz. of hand-rolling tobacco a month for as long as a year.)

□ 1   □ 2
YES   NO

6. Do you smoke cigarettes now? (at least 1 cigarette per day or 1 oz. of hand-rolling tobacco a month for the past year.)

□ 1   □ 2
YES   NO

7. How many cigarettes PER DAY and/or ounces of hand-rolling tobacco PER WEEK do you smoke?

□□   □
Cigs. / day   ozs./week

8. Do you smoke a pipe?

□ 1   □ 2
YES   NO

9. Do you smoke cigars?

□ 1   □ 2
YES   NO

10. Do you smoke ...

	YES	NO
....at school	□ 1	□ 2
...in front of pupils either in or out of the classroom	□ 1	□ 2
...out of school	□ 1	□ 2

AFTER COMPLETION COULD YOU PUT THIS QUESTIONNAIRE INSIDE THE ACCOMPANYING ENVELOPE, SEAL IT, AND LEAVE THIS IN YOUR SCHOOL SECRETARY'S OFFICE.

MANY THANKS FOR YOUR CO-OPERATION.

IF YOU HAVE ANY COMMENTS WOULD YOU PLEASE WRITE THEM BELOW.

153

CONFIDENTIAL

c.c. 1 2 3 4 5 6 7 8 9 10 11

| H | S | P | F | 7 | 4 | 06010 |

MEDICAL RESEARCH COUNCIL/DERBYSHIRE SMOKING STUDY
PARENTS' QUESTIONNAIRE

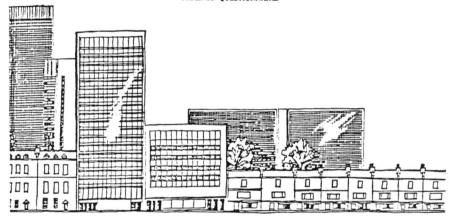

This questionnaire is divided into three sections. The first section, which is on blue paper, can be filled in by either parent or guardian. The second part of the questionnaire, on white paper, should be completed by the mother or female guardian only.

The third part of the questionnaire, on blue paper, should be completed by the father or male guardian only.

All your replies will be treated as strictly confidential.

```
┌─────────────────────────────────┐
│        FOR OFFICE USE ONLY       │
│                                  │
│   School number  ☐ ☐ ☐ ☐         │
└─────────────────────────────────┘
```

Please complete this form for _____

First name _____

_____

Section I This section may be completed by either parent or guardian.

What is the child's date of birth?   ☐ ☐   ☐ ☐   19 ☐ ☐
                                      date   month   year

Sex (please tick box)   Boy ☐ 1 Girl ☐ 2

1. Please give your relationship to him or her.

Mother or female guardian ☐ 1

Father or male guardian ☐ 2

We would like to ask some questions about your child's health. Please answer by ticking the appropriate box.

2a. Does he/she USUALLY cough first thing in the morning?
(exclude clearing throat or single cough)

YES ☐ 1   NO ☐ 2

2b. Does he/she USUALLY cough during the day or at night?
(exclude clearing throat or single cough)

YES ☐ 1   NO ☐ 2

3a. Does he/she USUALLY bring up any phlegm from the chest
first thing in the morning?

YES ☐ 1   NO ☐ 2

3b. Does he/she USUALLY bring up any phlegm from the chest
during the day or at night?

YES ☐ 1   NO ☐ 2

4. Do you notice that he/she is short of breath when playing
with other children?

YES ☐ 1   NO ☐ 2

If YES, do you think this is more than in other children
of the same age?

YES ☐ 1   NO ☐ 2

5. Has he/she ever suffered from any of the following? For each item
tick YES or NO.

	YES	NO
Asthma	☐ 1	☐ 2
Bronchitis	☐ 1	☐ 2
Wheezy chest	☐ 1	☐ 2
Pneumonia	☐ 1	☐ 2
Eczema	☐ 1	☐ 2
Hay fever (during the spring & summer months)	☐ 1	☐ 2
Hay fever (during the autumn & winter months)	☐ 1	☐ 2

156

6. How would you describe your child's health?

Very good ☐ 1

Good ☐ 2

Fair ☐ 3

Poor ☐ 4

---

7. IF THIS CHILD IS A GIRL

Has she started her monthly periods yet? YES ☐ 1 NO ☐ 2

If YES, when did they begin?
(please record the month as a number)
e.g. MARCH would be [0 3]   [   ] month   19 [   ] year

We would like to ask you some questions about the members of your household and their smoking habits, if any.

8. What is the total number of people, excluding this child, who live in your household?   [   ]

---

9. Of that total number, how many smoke cigarettes?   [   ]

---

10. Does this child live with:
(please tick one box only)

Both parents ☐ 1

Mother only ☐ 2

Father only ☐ 3

Foster parents ☐ 4

Others ☐ 5

157

Section II This section is to be completed by the mother or female guardian.

11. What is your relationship to this child? (please tick one box)

Mother ☐ 1

Female guardian ☐ 2

Other ☐ 3

12. At what age would you like this child to leave school?

☐☐ Years

13a. Have you ever smoked cigarettes? (i.e., at least 1
cigarette per day for as long as a year)

YES ☐ 1   NO ☐ 2

13b. Do you smoke now? (at least 1 cigarette per day
for the past year)

YES ☐ 1   NO ☐ 2

14. How many cigarettes do you smoke PER DAY?
(please write the amount in numbers)

☐☐

158

15. Here are some statements, opinions and ideas about smoking and school life. We would like you to tell us whether you agree or disagree with them. If you agree with a statement, put a tick by it in the column marked 'agree.' If you disagree, please tick the column marked 'disagree.' If you agree very much, tick the column marked 'strongly agree.' If you disagree very much, tick the column marked 'strongly disagree.' If you really can't make up your mind, tick the column marked 'dont know.' Put one tick in each row.

		Strongly Agree	Agree	Don't Know	Disagree	Strongly Disagree
1.	Smoking does more good for a person than harm	1	2	3	4	5
2.	Smoking is a dirty habit.	1	2	3	4	5
3.	Cigarettes should be less available to adolescents.	1	2	3	4	5
4.	I wouldn't like my children to smoke.	1	2	3	4	5
5.	I like to have a reasonably strong control over my child's behaviour.	1	2	3	4	5
6.	One can't tell how successful in life a person will be until they leave school.	1	2	3	4	5
7.	There is nothing wrong with smoking.	1	2	3	4	5
8.	Children should be discouraged from smoking.	1	2	3	4	5
9.	I don't allow my child to stay out late.	1	2	3	4	5
10.	I am satisfied with the education my child is receiving.	1	2	3	4	5
11.	Children should never smoke.	1	2	3	4	5
12.	Children at school should receive more health education telling them about problems of smoking and drinking.	1	2	3	4	5
13.	I try to discuss school work with my child.	1	2	3	4	5
14.	If children and adolescents want to smoke then there's nothing adults can do about it.	1	2	3	4	5
15.	In general, education helps people get on in the world.	1	2	3	4	5
16.	Smoking is pleasurable.	1	2	3	4	5
17.	Morally, no one should prevent someone else from smoking.	1	2	3	4	5

159

	Strongly Agree	Agree	Don't Know	Disagree	Strongly Disagree

18. There is not enough fuss being made about the dangers of smoking. ☐ 1 ☐ 2 ☐ 3 ☐ 4 ☐ 5

19. Once a teenager is allowed to smoke he will probably grow up to be a heavy smoker ☐ 1 ☐ 2 ☐ 3 ☐ 4 ☐ 5

20. Parents who smoke have no right to prevent their children from smoking. ☐ 1 ☐ 2 ☐ 3 ☐ 4 ☐ 5

21. I would encourage my child to take up some form of further education. ☐ 1 ☐ 2 ☐ 3 ☐ 4 ☐ 5

16a. If you are working at present could you describe your job, or if you are not working at present, your last job?

_____

_____

16b. In what industry, trade or profession is that job?

_____

16c. Are you or were you:

Self - employed ☐

An employer ☐

An employee ☐

Office Use ☐

Thank you very much for your help; this is the end of the mother's section.

160

17. What is your relationship to this child? (please tick one box)

Father ☐ 1

Male Guardian ☐ 2

Other ☐ 3

18. At what age would you like this child to leave school?

☐ Years

19a. Have you ever smoked cigarettes (i.e., at least 1 cigarette per day or 1 oz. of tobacco a month for as long as a year)

YES ☐ 1 NO ☐ 2

19b. Do you smoke cigarettes now? (at least 1 cigarette per day or 1 oz. of tobacco a month for the past year)

YES ☐ 1 NO ☐ 2

20a. How many cigarettes do you smoke PER DAY and/or ozs. of rolling tobacco PER WEEK (If you don't smoke put 0).

☐ cigs. ☐ ozs.

20b. Do you smoke a pipe or cigars?

YES ☐ 1 NO ☐ 2

161

21 Here are some statements, opinions and ideas about smoking and school life. We would like you to tell us whether you agree or disagree with them. If you agree with a statement, put a tick by it in the column marked 'agree'. If you disagree, please tick the column marked 'disagree'. If you agree very much, tick the column marked 'Strongly agree'. If you disagree very much, tick the column marked 'Strongly disagree'. If you really can't make up your mind, tick the column marked 'don't know'. Put one tick in each row.

		Strongly Agree	Agree	Don't Know	Disagree	Strongly Disagree
1.	Smoking does more good for a person than harm.	1	2	3	4	5
2.	Smoking is a dirty habit.	1	2	3	4	5
3.	Cigarettes should be less available to adolescents.	1	2	3	4	5
4.	I wouldn't like my children to smoke.	1	2	3	4	5
5.	I like to have a reasonably strong control over my child's behaviour.	1	2	3	4	5
6.	One can't tell how successful in life a person will be until they leave school.	1	2	3	4	5
7.	There is nothing wrong with smoking.	1	2	3	4	5
8.	Children should be discouraged from smoking.	1	2	3	4	5
9.	I don't allow my child to stay out late.	1	2	3	4	5
10.	I am satisfied with the education my child is receiving.	1	2	3	4	5
11.	Children should never smoke.	1	2	3	4	5
12.	Children at school should receive more health education telling them about problems of smoking and drinking.	1	2	3	4	5.
13.	I try to discuss school work with my child.	1	2	3	4	5
14.	If children and adolescents want to smoke then there's nothing adults can do about it.	1	2	3	4	5
15.	In general, education helps people get on in the world.	1	2	3	4	5
16.	Smoking is pleasurable.	1	2	3	4	5
17.	Morally, no one should prevent someone else from smoking.	1	2	3	4	5

		Strongly Agree	Agree	Don't Know	Disagree	Strongly Disagree
18.	There is not enough fuss being made about the dangers of smoking.	☐ 1	☐ 2	☐ 3	☐ 4	☐ 5
19.	Once a teenager is allowed to smoke he will probably grow up to be a heavy smoker.	☐ 1	☐ 2	☐ 3	☐ 4	☐ 5
20.	Parents who smoke have no right to prevent their children from smoking.	☐ 1	☐ 2	☐ 3	☐ 4	☐ 5
21.	I would encourage my child to take up some form of further education.	☐ 1	☐ 2	☐ 3	☐ 4	☐ 5

22a. If you are working at present could you describe your job, or if you are not working at present, your last job?

_____

_____

22b. In what industry, trade or profession is that job?

_____

22c. Are you or were you:

          Self - employed   ☐

          An employer   ☐

          An employee   ☐

Office Use

☐

Thank you very much for your help; this is the end of the questionnaire.

163

CONFIDENTIAL

c.c. 1 2 3 4 5 6 7 8 9 10 11

EACH CARD | H | S | P | C | 7 | S | 0 0 2 6 9 |

MRC/DERBYSHIRE SMOKING STUDY
SCHOOLCHILD QUESTIONNAIRE (2nd YEAR)

Your answers to these questions will help us to find out more about smoking and how it affects the health of young people. Please answer all the questions. All your replies will be strictly confidential. Your parents and teachers will not see them. They will be seen only by the medical research team.

When you have answered all the questions, please put this questionnaire in the envelope and seal it.

Now turn over the page and begin.

164

PLEASE WRITE IN BLOCK CAPITALS

YOUR LAST NAME _____

YOUR FIRST NAME(S) _____

WHAT IS YOUR DATE OF BIRTH?   Please write this in numbers. For example
1st June 1962 would be:-

| 0 , 1 | 0 , 6 | 19 6 , 2 |
| Date | Month | Year |

A guide to the number of each month is given for you:-

JAN	FEB	MAR	APR	MAY	JUNE	JULY	AUG	SEPT	OCT	NOV	DEC
0 , 1	0 , 2	0 , 3	0 , 4	0 , 5	0 , 6	0 , 7	0 , 8	0 , 9	1 , 0	1 , 1	1 , 2

NOW WRITE YOUR OWN DATE OF BIRTH
IN THESE BOXES .

| | | 19 |
| Date | Month | Year |

WHAT SEX ARE YOU? (Please tick one box)

BOY ☐ , GIRL ☐ ₂

WRITE THE FULL NAME OF YOUR SCHOOL _____

SCHOOL NUMBER (your teacher will tell you this)

| | | | |

WHAT FORM ARE YOU IN? _____

These first questions concern your health. Please make sure that you answer every question, whether you smoke or not.

---

1) a) Do you usually cough first thing in the morning?
(please tick one box)

Yes [ ] 1

No [ ] 2

b) Do you usually cough first thing in the morning like this for as much as three months each year?
(please tick one box)

Yes [ ] 1

No [ ] 2

---

2) a) Do you usually cough during the day or night?
(please tick one box)

Yes [ ] 1

No [ ] 2

b) Do you usually cough during the day or night like this for as much as three months each year?
(please tick one box)

Yes [ ] 1

No [ ] 2

---

3) Do you get short of breath when hurrying on flat ground or walking up a slight hill?
(please tick one box)

Yes [ ] 1

No [ ] 2

---

4) Please read these statements carefully and tick the one box which best describes you. (tick one box only)

I have never smoked a cigarette. [ ] 1

I have only ever tried smoking once. [ ] 2

I have smoked sometimes, but I don't smoke as much as one a week. [ ] 3

I usually smoke between one and six cigarettes a week. [ ] 4

I usually smoke more than six cigarettes a week. [ ] 5

---

5) Since this time last week how many cigarettes have you smoked?

(Write the figure in the box; if you haven't smoked any, write 0.)

[   ]

166

6)   I smoke with OTHER PEOPLE ....
     (tick one box only)

..... most of the time   ☐ 1

..... sometimes   ☐ 2

..... hardly ever   ☐ 3

I don't smoke   ☐ 4

7)   I smoke BY MYSELF ....
     (tick one box only)

..... most of the time   ☐ 1

..... sometimes   ☐ 2

..... hardly ever   ☐ 3

I don't smoke   ☐ 4

8) If you have EVER smoked a cigarette, we would like you to tell us why you did so.

If you have NEVER smoked, tick this box.

I HAVE NEVER SMOKED ☐ 1

If you have EVER smoked, please tick the sentences which describe why you started.
(Tick as many boxes as you like)

I smoked because my mother or father smokes ☐ 1

I smoked because my friends smoke ☐ 1

I smoked because I wanted to feel grown-up ☐ 1

I smoked because my brother or sister smokes ☐ 1

I smoked because I was dared to smoke ☐ 1

Please write in any other reason _____

_____

---

9) Does your father smoke cigarettes?
(please tick one box)

Yes ☐ 1

No ☐ 2

I don't know ☐ 3

I have no father ☐ 4

---

10) Does your father smoke a pipe or cigars?
(please tick one box)

Yes ☐ 1

No ☐ 2

I don't know ☐ 3

I have no father ☐ 4

168

11) Does your mother smoke cigarettes?
(please tick one box)

Yes ☐ 1

No ☐ 2

I don't know ☐ 3

I have no mother ☐ 4

12) How many brothers do you have? ☐

How many of them smoke cigarettes?
(Put figures in the boxes.) ☐

13) How many sisters do you have? ☐

How many of them smoke cigarettes?
(Put figures in the boxes.) ☐

14) How many of your friends IN THIS SCHOOL smoke cigarettes?
(please tick one box)

All of them ☐ 1

Most of them ☐ 2

Half of them ☐ 3

A few of them ☐ 4

None ☐ 5

169

15) How many of your friends WHO DON'T COME TO THIS SCHOOL smoke cigarettes?
(please tick one box)

All of them ☐ 1

Most of them ☐ 2

Half of them ☐ 3

A few of them ☐ 4

None ☐ 5

16) How many evenings a week do you USUALLY spend doing homework?
(please tick one box.)

5 or more evenings a week ☐ 1

3 or 4 evenings ☐ 2

1 or 2 evenings ☐ 3

No evenings ☐ 4

17) How many evenings a week do you USUALLY go out?
(please tick one box.)

5 or more evenings ☐ 1

3 or 4 evenings ☐ 2

1 or 2 evenings ☐ 3

No evenings ☐ 4

18) What kind of things do you do in your spare time?
(Tick as many boxes as you like.)

Sports and games ☐ 1

Go to the cinema ☐ 1

Scouts or Boys Brigade ☐ 1

Guides or Girls Brigade ☐ 1

Music or a hobby ☐ 1

Go dancing ☐ 1

Go around with a group of my own age ☐ 1

Watch T.V. or play records ☐ 1

Mess around ☐ 1

Go to a youth club ☐ 1

Read ☐ 1

Help out at home, in the house or on a farm ☐ 1

Anything else _____
(please describe)

19) With whom do you spend MOST of your spare time?
(please tick one or more boxes)

A group of boys ☐ 1

A group of girls ☐ 1

A boyfriend or girlfriend ☐ 1

A friend ☐ 1

A group of boys and girls ☐ 1

My parents ☐ 1

On my own ☐ 1

I don't go out much ☐ 1

Anything else _____
(please describe)

171

20) Do you have a part-time job outside school hours?
(please tick one box)

Yes ☐ 1   No ☐ 2

If YES, what kind of job is this? _____

_____

21) How much money PER WEEK do you spend on yourself?
(put the amount in figures)

£ ☐ ☐ p

22) How much money PER WEEK do you save?
(put the amount in figures)

£ ☐ ☐ p

23) Out of lesson time, what school teams, clubs or societies do you belong to?

Sports or games teams (e.g., football, hockey, chess) ☐ 1

Music ☐ 1

Drama ☐ 1

Art or handicraft ☐ 1

None ☐ 1

Anything else _____

_____

24) Have you played truant or skived from school?
(please tick one box)

Never ☐ 1

Once or twice ☐ 2

Sometimes ☐ 3

Often ☐ 4

172

25) Here are some statements, opinions and ideas about smoking and school life. We would like you to tell us whether you agree with them. If you agree with a statement, put a tick by it in the column marked "agree." If you disagree, please tick the column marked "disagree." If you agree very much, tick the column marked "strongly agree." If you disagree very much, tick the column marked "strongly disagree." If you really don't know whether you agree or disagree, tick the column marked "dont know."

Put one tick in each row.

For example, 'Parents don't understand the younger generation'. If you agree very much with this, you will tick the "strongly agree" column, like this:

	Strongly Agree	Agree	Don't Know	Disagree	Strongly Disagree
Parents don't understand the younger generation.	✓	☐	☐	☐	☐

Now do the same for each of the statements. Please read each one carefully before you answer. Remember one tick for each statement.

	Strongly Agree	Agree	Don't Know	Disagree	Strongly Disagree
1. Smoking can help people when they feel nervous or embarassed.	☐ 1	☐ 2	☐ 3	☐ 4	☐ 5
2. Most of my friends smoke cigarettes.	☐ 1	☐ 2	☐ 3	☐ 4	☐ 5
3. My parents are stricter than my teachers about smoking.	☐ 1	☐ 2	☐ 3	☐ 4	☐ 5
4. I am fed up with school.	☐ 1	☐ 2	☐ 3	☐ 4	☐ 5
5. My parents are upset if I do badly in my schoolwork.	☐ 1	☐ 2	☐ 3	☐ 4	☐ 5
6. Smoking is very enjoyable.	☐ 1	☐ 2	☐ 3	☐ 4	☐ 5
7. Smoking is dangerous only to older people.	☐ 1	☐ 2	☐ 3	☐ 4	☐ 5

173

		Strongly Agree	Agree	Don't Know	Disagree	Strongly Disagree
8.	A pupil who plays truant or skives from school should be punished.	1	2	3	4	5
9.	Cigarettes should be harder to get.	1	2	3	4	5
10.	Others make fun of you if you don't smoke.	1	2	3	4	5
·11.	Sometimes my brother or sister gives me a cigarette.	1	2	3	4	5
12.	My parents do not mind whom I go around with.	1	2	3	4	5
13.	Smoking is a dirty habit.	1	2	3	4	5
14.	Smoking is only bad for you if you smoke a lot.	1	2	3	4	5
15.	It is all right to tell a lie to a teacher to get out of trouble.	1	2	3	4	5
16.	You have to smoke when you're with friends who smoke.	1	2	3	4	5
17.	My parents don't allow me to smoke.	1	2	3	4	5
18.	My parents would like me to have a better job than my father's when I leave school.	1	2	3	4	5
19.	There is nothing wrong with copying from someone else in a school test.	1	2	3	4	5
20.	I would do what my friends want rather than what my parents want.	1	2	3	4	5
21.	Sometimes one of my parents gives me a cigarette.	1	2	3	4	5

174

		Strongly Agree	Agree	Don't Know	Disagree	Strongly Disagree
22.	I like boys and girls who fool around in class.	☐ 1	☐ 2	☐ 3	☐ 4	☐ 5
23.	Children caught smoking should be punished.	☐ 1	☐ 2	☐ 3	☐ 4	☐ 5
24.	Smoking is only bad for you if you have been smoking for many years.	☐ 1	☐ 2	☐ 3	☐ 4	☐ 5
25.	Pupils who look untidy in school should be told off.	☐ 1	☐ 2	☐ 3	☐ 4	☐ 5
26.	There is nothing wrong with smoking.	☐ 1	☐ 2	☐ 3	☐ 4	☐ 5
27.	Pupils should not be cheeky to the teacher.	☐ 1	☐ 2	☐ 3	☐ 4	☐ 5

This is the end of the questions. Now check to see that you have answered all the questions, and if you have any comments on the questionnaire write them in the space below.

Thank you very much.

CONFIDENTIAL

EACH CARD

c.c. 1 2 3 4 5 6 7 8 9 10 11

| H | S | P | C | 7 | 6 | 0 | 3 | 4 | 8 | 2 |

MRC/DERBYSHIRE SMOKING STUDY
PUPIL'S QUESTIONNAIRE (3rd YEAR)

We would like to thank you all for the help you have already given us in this study. We are interested in how people change their minds about smoking as they get older, so we would be grateful if you could fill in another questionnaire for us.

We would like to stress that your answers are CONFIDENTIAL and your parents and teachers have NOT and will NOT see any of the questionnaires.

Please answer ALL the questions. Put this in the envelope and seal it, and then hand it back to your teacher.

PLEASE WRITE IN BLOCK CAPITALS

YOUR LAST NAME _____

YOUR FIRST NAME(S) _____

WHAT IS YOUR DATE OF BIRTH? Please write this in numbers. For example 1st June 1962 would be:-

| 0 | 1 | | 0 | 6 | | 19 | 6 | 2 |

Date   Month   Year

A guide to the number of each month is given for you:-

JAN	FEB	MAR	APR	MAY	JUNE	JULY	AUG	SEPT	OCT	NOV	DEC
0 1	0 2	0 3	0 4	0 5	0 6	0 7	0 8	0 9	1 0	1 1	1 2

NOW WRITE YOUR OWN DATE OF BIRTH IN THESE BOXES .

[   ] [   ] 19 [   ]

Date   Month   Year

WHAT SEX ARE YOU? (Please tick one box)

BOY [ ]₁ GIRL [ ]₂

WRITE THE FULL NAME OF YOUR SCHOOL ....

WHAT FORM ARE YOU IN? ....

176

These first questions concern your health. Please make sure that you answer every question, whether you smoke or not.

1) Do you usually cough first thing in the morning?
(please tick one box)

YES ☐ 1

NO ☐ 2

2) Do you usually cough during the day or at night?
(Please tick one box)

YES ☐ 1

NO ☐ 2

3) Do you get short of breath when hurrying on flat ground or walking up a slight hill?
(please tick one box)

YES ☐ 1

NO ☐ 2

4) Does your chest ever sound wheezy or whistling during the day?
(please tick one box)

YES ☐ 1

NO ☐ 2

If YES–
Does your chest sound wheezy or whistling on most days?

YES ☐ 1

NO ☐ 2

5) Does your chest ever sound wheezy or whistling at night?
(please tick one box)

YES ☐ 1

NO ☐ 2

If YES–
Does your chest sound wheezy or whistling on most nights?

YES ☐ 1

NO ☐ 2

6) Have you ever been told that you had asthma?
(please tick one box)

YES ☐ 1

NO ☐ 2

7) What is meant by the term asthma?

Please write ....

....

177

8) Please read these statements carefully and tick the one box which best describes you. (tick one box only)

I have never smoked a cigarette. ☐ 1

I have only ever tried smoking once. ☐ 2

I have smoked sometimes, but I don't smoke as much as one a week. ☐ 3

I usually smoke between one and six cigarettes a week. ☐ 4

I usually smoke more than six cigarettes a week. ☐ 5

9) Since this time last week how many cigarettes have you smoked?

(write the figure in the box, e.g. 23 would be `2 3`

If you haven't smoked any write 0, like this `0`)

10) FOR SMOKERS

Which brands of cigarettes do you usually smoke?

Please write ....

11) Do you inhale and breathe the smoke right down into your lungs?
(please tick one box)

YES ☐ 1

NO ☐ 2

sometimes ☐ 3

I don't smoke ☐ 4

12) I smoke with OTHER PEOPLE ......
(tick one box only)

.... most of the time ☐ 1

.... sometimes ☐ 2

.... hardly ever ☐ 3

I don't smoke ☐ 4

178

13) I smoke BY MYSELF _____
(tick one box only)

_____ most of the time ☐ 1

_____ sometimes ☐ 2

_____ hardly ever ☐ 3

I don't smoke ☐ 4

14) If you have EVER smoked a cigarette, we would like you to tell us why you did so.

If you have NEVER smoked, tick this box: I HAVE NEVER SMOKED ☐ 1

If you have EVER smoked, please tick the sentences which describe why you started.
(Tick as many boxes as you like)

I smoked because my mother or father smokes ☐ 1

I smoked because because my friends smoke ☐ 1

I smoked because I wanted to feel grown-up ☐ 1

I smoked because my brother or sister smokes ☐ 1

I smoked because I was dared to smoke ☐ 1

I smoked because I wanted to see what it was like ☐ 1

Please write in any other reason _____

_____

15) Does your father smoke cigarettes?
(please tick one box)

Yes ☐ 1

No ☐ 2

I don't know ☐ 3

I have no father ☐ 4

179

16) Does your father smoke a pipe or cigars?
(please tick one box)

Yes ☐ 1

No ☐ 2

I don't know ☐ 3

I have no father ☐ 4

17) Does your mother smoke cigarettes?
(please tick one box)

Yes ☐ 1

No ☐ 2

I don't know ☐ 3

I have no mother ☐ 4

18) How many brothers do you have?

☐

How many of them smoke cigarettes?
(Put figures in the boxes.)

☐

19) How many sisters do you have?

☐

How many of them smoke cigarettes?
(Put figures in the boxes.)

☐

20) How many of your friends IN THIS SCHOOL smoke cigarettes?
(please tick one box)

All of them ☐ 1

Most of them ☐ 2

Half of them ☐ 3

A few of them ☐ 4

None ☐ 5

I don't know ☐ 6

21) How many of your friends WHO DON'T COME TO THIS SCHOOL smoke cigarettes?
(please tick one box)

All of them ☐ 1

Most of them ☐ 2

Half of them ☐ 3

A few of them ☐ 4

None ☐ 5

I don't know ☐ 6

22) How many evenings a week do you USUALLY spend doing homework?
(please tick one box.)

5 or more evenings a week ☐ 1

3 or 4 evenings ☐ 2

1 or 2 evenings ☐ 3

No evenings ☐ 4

23) How many evenings a week do you USUALLY go out?
(please tick one box.)

5 or more evenings ☐ 1

3 or 4 evenings ☐ 2

1 or 2 evenings ☐ 3

No evenings ☐ 4

181

24) What kind of things do you do in your spare time?
(Tick as many boxes as you like.)

Sports and games	☐ 1
Go to the cinema	☐ 1
Scouts or Boys Brigade	☐ 1
Guides or Girls Brigade	☐ 1
Music or a hobby	☐ 1
Go dancing	☐ 1
Go around with a group of my own age	☐ 1
Watch T.V.	☐ 1
Play records	☐ 1
Mess around	☐ 1
Go to a youth club	☐ 1
Read	☐ 1
Help out at home, in the house or on a farm	☐ 1

Anything else (please describe) ....

25) With whom do you spend MOST of your spare time?
(please tick one or more boxes)

A group of boys	☐ 1
A group of girls	☐ 1
A boyfriend or girlfriend	☐ 1
A friend	☐ 1
A group of boys and girls	☐ 1
My parents	☐ 1
On my own	☐ 1
I don't go out much	☐ 1

Anyone else ....
(please describe)

182

26) Do you have a part-time job outside school hours?
(please tick one box)

Yes ☐ 1   No ☐ 2

If YES, what kind of job is this? _____
_____

27) How much money PER WEEK do you spend on yourself?
(put the amount in figures)

£ ☐☐ p

28) How much money PER WEEK do you spend on cigarettes?
(put the amount in figures)

£ ☐☐ p

29) Out of lesson time, what school teams, clubs or societies do you belong to?

Sports or games teams (e.g., football, hockey, swimming, chess) ☐ 1

Music ☐ 1

Drama ☐ 1

Art or handicraft ☐ 1

Anything else _____
_____   None ☐ 1

30) In the past year have you played truant or skived from school?
(please tick one box)

Never ☐ 1

Once or twice ☐ 2

Sometimes ☐ 3

Often ☐ 4

31) Here are some statements, opinions and ideas about smoking and school life. Some of them are the same as you completed last year. This is because we are interested in how pupils' attitudes change from year to year. This year there are also some new items.

If you agree with a statement, put a tick by it in the column marked "agree". If you disagree, please tick the column marked "disagree". If you agree very much, tick the column marked "strongly agree". If you disagree very much tick the column marked "strongly disagree". If you really don't know whether you agree or disagree, tick the column marked "don't know".

Put one tick in each row.

For example, "Smoking should be banned". If you agree very much with this, you will tick the "strongly agree" column, like this.

	Strongly Agree	Agree	Don't Know	Disagree	Strongly Disagree
"Smoking should be banned"	✓	☐	☐	☐	☐

Now do the same for each of the statements. Please read each one carefully before you answer. Remember one tick for each statement.

	Strongly Agree	Agree	Don't Know	Disagree	Strongly Disagree
1. I like boys and girls who fool around in class.	☐ 1	☐ 2	☐ 3	☐ 4	☐ 5
2. Children caught smoking should be punished.	☐ 1	☐ 2	☐ 3	☐ 4	☐ 5
3. Smoking is only bad for you if you have been smoking for many years.	☐ 1	☐ 2	☐ 3	☐ 4	☐ 5
4. Pupils who look untidy in school should be told off.	☐ 1	☐ 2	☐ 3	☐ 4	☐ 5
5. There is nothing wrong with smoking.	☐ 1	☐ 2	☐ 3	☐ 4	☐ 5
6. Pupils should not be cheeky to the teacher.	☐ 1	☐ 2	☐ 3	☐ 4	☐ 5

		Strongly Agree	Agree	Don't Know	Disagree	Strongly Disagree

7. Smoking can help people when they feel nervous or embarassed. □ 1 □ 2 □ 3 □ 4 □ 5

8. Most of my friends smoke cigarettes. □ 1 □ 2 □ 3 □ 4 □ 5

9. My parents are stricter than my teachers about smoking. □ 1 □ 2 □ 3 □ 4 □ 5

10. I am fed up with school. □ 1 □ 2 □ 3 □ 4 □ 5

11. Smoking is very enjoyable. □ 1 □ 2 □ 3 □ 4 □ 5

12. Smoking is dangerous only to older people. □ 1 □ 2 □ 3 □ 4 □ 5

13. A pupil who plays truant or skives from school should be punished. □ 1 □ 2 □ 3 □ 4 □ 5

14. Cigarettes should be harder to get. □ 1 □ 2 □ 3 □ 4 □ 5

15. Others make fun of you if you don't smoke. □ 1 □ 2 □ 3 □ 4 □ 5

16. Sometimes my brother or sister gives me a cigarette. □ 1 □ 2 □ 3 □ 4 □ 5

17. Smoking is a dirty habit. □ 1 □ 2 □ 3 □ 4 □ 5

18. Smoking is only bad for you if you smoke a lot. □ 1 □ 2 □ 3 □ 4 □ 5

19. It is all right to tell a lie to a teacher to get out of trouble. □ 1 □ 2 □ 3 □ 4 □ 5

20. You have to smoke when you're with friends who smoke. □ 1 □ 2 □ 3 □ 4 □ 5

21. My parents don't allow me to smoke. □ 1 □ 2 □ 3 □ 4 □ 5

		Strongly Agree	Agree	Don't Know	Disagree	Strongly Disagree
22.	There is nothing wrong with copying from someone else in a school test.	☐ 1	☐ 2	☐ 3	☐ 4	☐ 5
23.	I would do what my friends want rather than what my parents want.	☐ 1	☐ 2	☐ 3	☐ 4	☐ 5
24.	Sometimes one of my parents gives me a cigarette.	☐ 1	☐ 2	☐ 3	☐ 4	☐ 5

This is the end of the questions. Now check to see that you have answered all the questions, and if you have any comments on the questionnaire write them in the space below.

Thank you very much.

CONFIDENTIAL

c.c.	1	2	3	4	5	6	7	8	9	10	11
EACH CARD	H	S	P	C	7	7					

MRC/DERBYSHIRE SMOKING STUDY
PUPIL'S QUESTIONNAIRE (4th YEAR)

We would like to thank you all for the help you have already given us in this study. We are interested in how people change their minds about smoking as they get older, so we would be grateful if you could fill in another questionnaire for us. There are some new questions this year.

We would like to stress again that your answers are CONFIDENTIAL and your parents and teachers have NOT and will NOT see any of the questionnaires.

Please answer ALL the questions. Don't forget to put this in the envelope and seal it, and then hand it back to your teacher.

PLEASE WRITE IN BLOCK CAPITALS

YOUR LAST NAME ....

YOUR FIRST NAME(S) ....

WHAT IS YOUR DATE OF BIRTH?   Please write this in numbers. For example 1st June 1962 would be:

0 1	0 6	19 6 2
Date	Month	Year

A guide to the number of each month is given for you:

JAN	FEB	MAR	APR	MAY	JUNE	JULY	AUG	SEPT	OCT	NOV	DEC
0 1	0 2	0 3	0 4	0 5	0 6	0 7	0 8	0 9	1 0	1 1	1 2

NOW WRITE YOUR OWN DATE OF BIRTH IN THESE BOXES.

		19
Date	Month	Year

WHAT SEX ARE YOU? (Please tick one box)

BOY [ ] 1   GIRL [ ] 2

WRITE THE FULL NAME OF YOUR SCHOOL ....

WHAT FORM ARE YOU IN? ....

187

These first questions concern your health. Please make sure that you answer every question, whether you smoke or not.

---

1) In general, would you say that you worry about your health?
(Please tick one box)

A great deal	☐ 1
Same as most people	☐ 2
Just a little	☐ 3
Not at all	☐ 4

---

2) How serious do you think the following diseases are?
(Please tick one box for each disease)

	Not serious	Fairly serious	Very serious
Bronchitis	☐ 1	☐ 2	☐ 3
Polio	☐ 1	☐ 2	☐ 3
Lung cancer	☐ 1	☐ 2	☐ 3
Influenza	☐ 1	☐ 2	☐ 3
Coronary heart disease	☐ 1	☐ 2	☐ 3

---

3) Which of the following is most harmful to one's health?
(Please tick just one box)

Being overweight	☐ 1
Not getting exercise	☐ 2
Smoking	☐ 3
Eating sweets	☐ 4
Not wearing a seat belt in a car	☐ 5

For this question tick one box for each statement.

4) Compared to smokers, do your think non-smokers ...

	Yes	No
... are healthier	☐ 1	☐ 2
... live longer	☐ 1	☐ 2
... are less attractive	☐ 1	☐ 2
... stay fitter	☐ 1	☐ 2
... have less days off school work	☐ 1	☐ 2
... do better in examinations	☐ 1	☐ 2

188

5) a) Do you usually cough first thing in the morning:
(Please tick one box)

Yes ☐ 1

No ☐ 2

b) Do you usually cough during the day or at night?
(Please tick one box)

Yes ☐ 1

No ☐ 2

If 'Yes' to either question (a) or (b):

c) Do you cough like this on most days for as much as
three months each year?

Yes ☐ 1

No ☐ 2

Does not apply ☐ 8

6) When you cough do you usually bring up phlegm (spit)?

Yes ☐ 1

No ☐ 2

7) Do you often suffer from a cold?
(Please tick one box)

Yes ☐ 1

No ☐ 2

8) When you get a cold, do you usually cough up phlegm (spit)?
(Please tick one box)

Yes ☐ 1

No ☐ 2

9) Do you get short of breath when hurrying on flat ground or
walking up a slight hill?
(Please tick one box)

Yes ☐ 1

No ☐ 2

189

10) Please read these statements carefully and tick the one which best describes you. (tick one box only)

I have never smoked a cigarette. ☐ 1

I have only ever tried smoking once. ☐ 2

I have smoked sometimes, but I don't smoke as much as one a week. ☐ 3

I usually smoke between one and six cigarettes a week. ☐ 4

I usually smoke more than six cigarettes a week. ☐ 5

I used to smoke but I have given it up. ☐ 6

---

11) Since this time last week how many cigarettes have you smoked?

(Write the figure in the box, e.g. 23 would be | 2 | 3 |

If you haven't smoked any write 0, like this | 0 |)

---

12) FOR SMOKERS

Which brands of cigarettes do you usually smoke?

Please write ....

....

---

13) Do you inhale and breathe the smoke right down into your lungs?
(Please tick one box)

Yes ☐ 1

Sometimes ☐ 2

No ☐ 3

I don't smoke ☐ 4

---

14) Which of the following members of your household at present smoke cigarettes?
(Tick one box on each row)

	Yes	No		
Father	☐ 1	☐ 2	I have no father	☐ 4
Mother	☐ 1	☐ 2	I have no mother	☐ 4
One or more brothers	☐ 1	☐ 2	I have no brothers	☐ 4
One or more sisters	☐ 1	☐ 2	I have no sisters	☐ 4

---

15) How many of your friends smoke cigarettes?

Most of them ☐ 1

Some of them ☐ 2

None ☐ 3

190

16) How many evenings a week do you USUALLY spend doing homework?
   (Please tick one box)

5 or more evenings a week	☐ 1
3 or 4 evenings	☐ 2
1 or 2 evenings	☐ 3
No evenings	☐ 4

17) How many evenings a week do you USUALLY go out?
   (Please tick one box)

5 or more evenings	☐ 1
3 or 4 evenings	☐ 2
1 or 2 evenings	☐ 3
No evenings	☐ 4

18) Do you have a part-time job?
   (Please tick one box)

   Yes ☐ 1   No ☐ 2

   If YES, what kind of job is this? ....
   ....

19) How much money do you have to spend per week?
   (Put the amount in figures)

   £ ☐☐ p

20) How much money do you spend on cigarettes per week?
   (Put the amount in figures)

   £ ☐☐ p

21) In the past year have you played truant or skived from school?
   (Please tick one box)

Never	☐ 1
Once or twice	☐ 2
Sometimes	☐ 3
Often	☐ 4

22) a) Have you ever had an alcoholic drink, e.g. beer, wine, whisky, cider, vodka?
(Please tick one box)

Yes ☐ 1

No ☐ 2

b) If 'Yes' how old were you when you first tasted an alcoholic drink?

☐☐ Number of years old

If 'No' put ☐ 0 0 ☐

23) When did you last have an alcoholic drink?
(Please tick one box)

In the last week ☐ 1

Over one week ago but less than one month ago ☐ 2

Over one month ago but less than 6 months ago ☐ 3

Over 6 months ago ☐ 4

I have never had an alcoholic drink ☐ 5

24) If you had a drink during the last week, please write down the number of drinks you have had in the past week, and what they were (e.g. one pint of cider, and two half pints of beer).

25) Where did you mainly drink these?
(Please tick one box)

At home ☐ 1

At a friend's house ☐ 2

In a pub ☐ 3

In a restaurant ☐ 4

Somewhere else ☐ 5

I don't drink ☐ 8

If 'Somewhere else' please write where:

192

26) At what age do you think you are most likely to leave school?
(Please tick one box)

16	☐	1
17	☐	2
18 or over	☐	3
Uncertain	☐	4

27) Do you consider yourself to be ...
(Please tick one box)

... underweight?	☐	1
... normal weight?	☐	2
... overweight?	☐	3

28) What special things do you do to try to keep healthy?

----

29) Here are some statements, opinions and ideas about health and smoking. We would like you to tell us whether you agree them. If you agree with a statement, put a tick by it in the column marked "agree". If you disagree, please tick the column marked "disagree". If you agree very much, tick the column marked "strongly agree". If you disagree very much, tick the column marked "strongly disagree". If you really don't know whether you agree or disagree, tick the column marked "don't know".

Put one tick in each row.

For example, 'Parliament should be reformed'. If you very much agree with this, you will tick the "strongly agree" column like this.

	Strongly Agree	Agree	Don't Know	Disagree	Strongly Disagree
Parliament should be reformed	☑	☐	☐	☐	☐

Now do the same for each statement. Please read each one carefully before you answer. Remember one tick for each statement.

	Strongly Agree	Agree	Don't Know	Disagree	Strongly Disagree
1. Cigarettes should be harder to get.	☐ 1	☐ 2	☐ 3	☐ 4	☐ 5
2. Smoking is only bad for you if you have been smoking for many years.	☐ 1	☐ 2	☐ 3	☐ 4	☐ 5
3. With common illnesses, old-fashioned remedies are still better than things doctors prescribe.	☐ 1	☐ 2	☐ 3	☐ 4	☐ 5
4. Smoking is a dirty habit.	☐ 1	☐ 2	☐ 3	☐ 4	☐ 5
5. Most of what happens to your health is a matter of chance.	☐ 1	☐ 2	☐ 3	☐ 4	☐ 5

193

	Strongly Agree	Agree	Don't Know	Disagree	Strongly Disagree
6. There are many things you can do to be healthy and avoid illness.	☐ 1	☐ 2	☐ 3	☐ 4	☐ 5
7. If I got sick it would be very bad for my family.	☐ 1	☐ 2	☐ 3	☐ 4	☐ 5
8. There is nothing wrong with smoking.	☐ 1	☐ 2	☐ 3	☐ 4	☐ 5
9. Smoking is dangerous only to older people.	☐ 1	☐ 2	☐ 3	☐ 4	☐ 5
10. Smoking is very enjoyable.	☐ 1	☐ 2	☐ 3	☐ 4	☐ 5
11. Children caught smoking should be punished.	☐ 1	☐ 2	☐ 3	☐ 4	☐ 5
12. Others make fun of you if you don't smoke.	☐ 1	☐ 2	☐ 3	☐ 4	☐ 5
13. Children do pretty well by themselves without being warned by parents to avoid colds and injuries.	☐ 1	☐ 2	☐ 3	☐ 4	☐ 5
14. Whenever I read or hear about some disease, I think I might get it.	☐ 1	☐ 2	☐ 3	☐ 4	☐ 5
15. Most of my friends smoke cigarettes.	☐ 1	☐ 2	☐ 3	☐ 4	☐ 5
16. I am fed up with school.	☐ 1	☐ 2	☐ 3	☐ 4	☐ 5
17. You have to smoke when you're with friends who smoke.	☐ 1	☐ 2	☐ 3	☐ 4	☐ 5
18. Sometimes my brother or sister gives me a cigarette.	☐ 1	☐ 2	☐ 3	☐ 4	☐ 5
19. Smoking is only bad for you if you smoke a lot.	☐ 1	☐ 2	☐ 3	☐ 4	☐ 5
20. Smoking can help people when they feel nervous or embarassed.	☐ 1	☐ 2	☐ 3	☐ 4	☐ 5
21. My parents don't allow me to smoke.	☐ 1	☐ 2	☐ 3	☐ 4	☐ 5
22. Sometimes one of my parents gives me a cigarette.	☐ 1	☐ 2	☐ 3	☐ 4	☐ 5
23. If you wait long enough, you will get over most illnesses.	☐ 1	☐ 2	☐ 3	☐ 4	☐ 5
24. We live in a time when there is more danger from diseases and accidents than ever before.	☐ 1	☐ 2	☐ 3	☐ 4	☐ 5

This is the end of the questions. Now check to see that you have answered all the questions, and if you have any comments on the questionnaire write them in the space below.
Thank you very much.

194

e.c. 1 2 3 4 5 6 7 8 9 10 11

EACH CARD | H | S | P | C | 7 | 8 | 0 6 2 7 0 |

MRC/DERBYSHIRE SMOKING STUDY
PUPIL'S QUESTIONNAIRE (5th YEAR)

Thank you for all the help you have given us in this five year study. This is the last time we shall be asking you to complete a questionnaire. Your answers are helping us to find out more about cigarette smoking, the views of young people, and if smoking affects the health of young people.

Please answer ALL questions; your replies are CONFIDENTIAL and your parents and teachers have NOT and will not be shown your answers.

PLEASE WRITE IN BLOCK CAPITALS

YOUR LAST NAME _____

YOUR FIRST NAME(S) _____

WHAT IS YOUR DATE OF BIRTH?   Please write this in numbers. For example
1st June 1962 would be:

0	1		0	6		19	6	2
Date			Month				Year	

A guide to the number of each month is given for you:

JAN	FEB	MAR	APR	MAY	JUNE	JULY	AUG	SEPT	OCT	NOV	DEC
0 1	0 2	0 3	0 4	0 5	0 6	0 7	0 8	0 9	1 0	1 1	1 2

NOW WRITE YOUR OWN DATE OF BIRTH
IN THESE BOXES.

				19		
Date		Month			Year	

WHAT SEX ARE YOU? (Please tick one box)

BOY [ ]₁   GIRL [ ]₂

WRITE THE FULL NAME OF YOUR SCHOOL _____

WHAT FORM ARE YOU IN? _____

195

These first questions concern your health. Please make sure that you answer every question, whether you smoke or not.

1) In general, would you say that you worry about your health?
(Please tick one box)

A great deal ☐ 1

Same as most people ☐ 2

Just a little ☐ 3

Not at all ☐ 4

2) How serious do you think the following diseases are?
(Please tick one box for each disease)

	Not serious	Fairly serious	Very serious
Bronchitis	☐ 1	☐ 2	☐ 3
Polio	☐ 1	☐ 2	☐ 3
Lung cancer	☐ 1	☐ 2	☐ 3
Influenza	☐ 1	☐ 2	☐ 3
Coronary heart disease	☐ 1	☐ 2	☐ 3

3) Which of the following is most harmful to one's health?
(Please tick just one box)

Being overweight ☐ 1

Not getting exercise ☐ 2

Smoking ☐ 3

Eating sweets ☐ 4

Not wearing a seat belt in a car ☐ 5

For this question tick one box for each statement.

4) Compared to smokers, do you think non-smokers ...

	Yes	No
... are healthier	☐ 1	☐ 2
... live longer	☐ 1	☐ 2
... are less attractive	☐ 1	☐ 2
... stay fitter	☐ 1	☐ 2
... have less days off school	☐ 1	☐ 2
... do better in examinations	☐ 1	☐ 2

196

5) a) Do you usually cough first thing in the morning:
   (Please tick one box)

   Yes ☐ 1

   No ☐ 2

   b) Do you usually cough during the day or at night?
   (Please tick one box)

   Yes ☐ 1

   No ☐ 2

   If 'Yes' to either question (a) or (b):

   c) Do you cough like this on most days for as much as
   three months each year?

   Yes ☐ 1

   No ☐ 2

   Does not apply ☐ 8

6) When you cough do you usually bring up phlegm (spit)?
   (Please tick one box)

   Yes ☐ 1

   No ☐ 2

7) Do you often suffer from a cold?
   (Please tick one box)

   Yes ☐ 1

   No ☐ 2

8) When you get a cold, do you usually cough up phlegm (spit)?
   (Please tick one box)

   Yes ☐ 1

   No ☐ 2

9) Do you get short of breath when hurrying on flat ground or
   walking up a slight hill?
   (Please tick one box)

   Yes ☐ 1

   No ☐ 2

197

10) Since last September how many days have you been
absent from school?
(Please tick one box)

None	☐ 1
1-4 days	☐ 2
5-9 days	☐ 3
10-14 days	☐ 4
More than 3 weeks	☐ 5

If you have been absent, was this mostly because of . . .

Coughs and colds	☐ 1
Accidents (broken bones etc.)	☐ 2
Other sickness	☐ 3
No particular reasons	☐ 4
Other (please state)	☐ 6

11) Please read these statements carefully and tick the one which best
describes you. (tick one box only)

I have never smoked a cigarette.	☐ 1
I have only ever tried smoking once.	☐ 2
I have smoked sometimes, but I don't smoke as much as one a week.	☐ 3
I usually smoke between one and six cigarettes a week.	☐ 4
I usually smoke more than six cigarettes a week.	☐ 5
I used to smoke but I have given it up.	☐ 6

12a) Since this time last week how many cigarettes have you smoked?

(Write the figure in the box, e.g. 23 would be [2 | 3]

If you haven't smoked any write 0, like this [0])

12b) For Smokers
Which brand of cigarettes do you usually smoke?
(Please tick one box)

Players Number 6 Filter Tip	☐ 22
Players Number 10 Filter Tip	☐ 09
Embassy Filter Tip	☐ 52
Embassy Regal	☐ 20
Silk Cut	☐ 11
Any other brands write in full	☐☐

198

13) Do you inhale and breathe the smoke right down into your lungs?
(Please tick one box)

Yes ☐ 1

Sometimes ☐ 2

No ☐ 3

I don't smoke ☐ 4

14) Which of the following members of your household at present smoke cigarettes?
(Tick one box on each row)

	Yes	No		
Father	☐ 1	☐ 2	I have no father	☐ 4
Mother	☐ 1	☐ 2	I have no mother	☐ 4
One or more brothers	☐ 1	☐ 2	I have no brothers	☐ 4
One or more sisters	☐ 1	☐ 2	I have no sisters	☐ 4

15) How many of your friends smoke cigarettes?

Most of them ☐ 1

Some of them ☐ 2

None ☐ 3

16a) Does your father allow you to smoke?

Yes ☐ 1

No ☐ 2

I have no father ☐ 4

b) Does your mother allow you to smoke?

Yes ☐ 1

No ☐ 3

I have no mother ☐ 4

17) How many evenings a week do you USUALLY spend doing homework?
(Please tick one box)

5 or more evenings a week ☐ 1

3 or 4 evenings ☐ 2

1 or 2 evenings ☐ 3

No evenings ☐ 4

18) How many evenings a week do you USUALLY go out?
(Please tick one box)

5 or more evenings ☐ 1

3 or 4 evenings ☐ 2

1 or 2 evenings ☐ 3

No evenings ☐ 4

199

19) Do you have a part-time job?
(Please tick one box)

Yes ☐ 1   No ☐ 2

If YES, please tick the kind
of job you do

Paper round ☐ 1

Babysitting ☐ 2

Shop work ☐ 3

Farm work ☐ 4

Door-to-door/milk round ☐ 6

Voluntary work ☐ 8

Other paid work ☐ 7

Please specify _____

20) How much money do you have for spending per week?
(Put the amount in figures)

£ ☐ ☐ p

21) How much money do you spend on cigarettes per week?
(Put the amount in figures)

£ ☐ ☐ p

22) In the past year have you played truant or skived from school?
(Please tick one box)

Never ☐ 1

Once or twice ☐ 2

Sometimes ☐ 3

Often ☐ 4

23) How do you usually travel between home and school?
(Please tick one box in each column)

	Home to School	School to Home
School BUS	☐ 1	☐ 1
Public transport	☐ 2	☐ 2
Car	☐ 3	☐ 3
On foot	☐ 4	☐ 4
Bike	☐ 5	☐ 5
Other _____	☐ 6	☐ 6

200

24a) Have you ever had an alcoholic drink, e.g. beer, wine, whisky, cider, vodka?
    (Please tick one box)

    Yes ☐
    No ☐ 5

b) If 'Yes' to question 24a, when did you last have one?
    (Please tick one box)

    In the last week ☐ 1

    Over one week ago but less than one month ago ☐ 2

    Over one month ago but less than 6 months ago ☐ 3

    Over 6 months ago ☐ 4

---

25) If you had a drink during the last week, please write down the number of drinks you have had and what they were (e.g. one pint of cider, and two half pints of beer).

    _____

---

26) Where did you mainly drink these?
    (Please tick one box)

    At home ☐ 1

    At a friend's house ☐ 2

    In a pub ☐ 3

    In a restaurant ☐ 4

    Somewhere else ☐ 5

    Club ☐ 6

    Disco ☐ 7

    I don't drink ☐ 8

If 'Somewhere else', please write where:

    _____

---

27) At what age do you think you are most likely to leave full-time education?
    Please tick one box)

    16 ☐ 1

    17 ☐ 2

    18 or over ☐ 3

    I intend to go on to college/university ☐ 4

---

28) What job or occupation do you hope to do when you have finished your full-time education?

    _____

29) What special things do you do to try to keep healthy? (General health and dental care).

----

30) Here are some statements, opinions and ideas about health and smoking. We would like you to tell us whether you agree with them. If you agree with a statement, put a tick by it in the column marked "agree". If you disagree please tick the column marked "disagree". If you agree very much, tick the column marked "strongly agree". If you disagree very much, tick the column marked "strongly disagree". If you really don't know whether you agree or disagree, tick the column marked "don't know".

Put one tick in each row.

For example, 'Parliament should be reformed'. If you agree with this but don't strongly agree, tick the 'Agree' column like this:

	Strongly Agree	Agree	Don't Know	Disagree	Strongly Disagree
Parliament should be reformed	☐	☑	☐	☐	☐

Now do the same for each statement. Please read each one carefully before you answer. Remember one tick for each statement.

	Strongly Agree	Agree	Don't Know	Disagree	Strongly Disagree
1. Cigarettes should be harder to get.	☐ 1	☐ 2	☐ 3	☐ 4	☐ 5
2. Smoking is only bad for you if you have been smoking for many years.	☐ 1	☐ 2	☐ 3	☐ 4	☐ 5
3. With common illnesses, old-fashioned remedies are still better than things doctors prescribe.	☐ 1	☐ 2	☐ 3	☐ 4	☐ 5
4. Smoking is a dirty habit.	☐ 1	☐ 2	☐ 3	☐ 4	☐ 5
5. Most of what happens to your health is a matter of chance.	☐ 1	☐ 2	☐ 3	☐ 4	☐ 5
6. There are many things you can do to be healthy and avoid illness.	☐ 1	☐ 2	☐ 3	☐ 4	☐ 5
7. There is nothing wrong with smoking.	☐ 1	☐ 2	☐ 3	☐ 4	☐ 5
8. Smoking is dangerous only to older people.	☐ 1	☐ 2	☐ 3	☐ 4	☐ 5
9. Smoking is very enjoyable.	☐ 1	☐ 2	☐ 3	☐ 4	☐ 5
10. Children caught smoking should be punished.	☐ 1	☐ 2	☐ 3	☐ 4	☐ 5
11. Others make fun of you if you don't smoke.	☐ 1	☐ 2	☐ 3	☐ 4	☐ 5
12. Children do pretty well by themselves without being warned by parents to avoid colds and injuries.	☐ 1	☐ 2	☐ 3	☐ 4	☐ 5

	Strongly Agree	Agree	Don't Know	Disagree	Strongly Disagree
13. Whenever I read or hear about some disease, I think I might get it.	☐ 1	☐ 2	☐ 3	☐ 4	☐ 5
14. I am fed up with school.	☐ 1	☐ 2	☐ 3	☐ 4	☐ 5
15. You have to smoke when you're with friends who smoke.	☐ 1	☐ 2	☐ 3	☐ 4	☐ 5
16. Smoking is only bad for you if you smoke a lot.	☐ 1	☐ 2	☐ 3	☐ 4	☐ 5
17. Smoking can help people when they feel nervous or embarrassed.	☐ 1	☐ 2	☐ 3	☐ 4	☐ 5
18. If you wait long enough, you will get over most illnesses.	☐ 1	☐ 2	☐ 3	☐ 4	☐ 5
19. We live in a time when there is more danger from diseases and accidents than ever before.	☐ 1	☐ 2	☐ 3	☐ 4	☐ 5
20. If a woman smokes when she is pregnant, it may harm her baby.	☐ 1	☐ 2	☐ 3	☐ 4	☐ 5

What do you think makes young people take up smoking?

....

....

....

This is the end of the questions. Now check to see that you have answered all the questions, and if you have any comments on the questionnaire write them in the space below. When you have finished please fold the questionnaire, put it in the envelope and seal it, and hand it back to your teacher.

MEDICAL RESEARCH COUNCIL/DERBYSHIRE SMOKING SURVEY
PARENT QUESTIONNAIRE

All your replies will be treated as confidential.

1	2	3	4	5	6	7	8	9	10	11
H	S	P	F	?	8	1	0	8	0	2

Please complete this form for _____

First name _____

What is the child's date of birth? [ ][ ] [ ][ ] 19[ ][ ]

Sex (please tick box)   Boy [ ] 1 Girl [ ] 2

This questionnaire should be completed by the mother or female guardian.

If child lives with father/male guardian only please tick here and continue. [ ]

FOR OFFICE USE ONLY
[ ][ ][ ][ ]

would like to ask some questions about your child's health. Please answer by ticking the appropriate box.

	Yes	No
1a. Does he/she USUALLY cough first thing in the morning? (exclude clearing throat or single cough)	[ ] 1	[ ] 2
1b. Does he/she USUALLY cough during the day or at night? (exclude clearing throat or single cough)	[ ] 1	[ ] 2

	Yes	No
2a. Does he/she USUALLY bring up any phlegm from the chest first thing in the morning?	[ ] 1	[ ] 2
2b. Does he/she USUALLY bring up any phlegm from the chest during the day or night?	[ ] 1	[ ] 2

	Yes	No
3. Do you notice that he/she is short of breath when playing with other children?	[ ] 1	[ ] 2
If YES do you think this is more than in other children of the same age.	[ ] 1	[ ] 2

4. Has he/she suffered from any of these in the last two years? Please tick 'YES' or 'NO' for each item.

	Yes	No
Asthma	[ ] 1	[ ] 2
Bronchitis	[ ] 1	[ ] 2
Wheezy chest	[ ] 1	[ ] 2
Pneumonia	[ ] 1	[ ] 2
Eczema	[ ] 1	[ ] 2
Hay fever (during the spring and summer months)	[ ] 1	[ ] 2
Hay fever (during the autumn and winter months)	[ ] 1	[ ] 2

204

5. How would you describe your child's health?

Very good ☐ 1   Good ☐ 2   Fair ☐ 3   Poor ☐ 4

---

6. In the past two years has he/she been admitted to hospital?

	Yes	No
	☐ 1	☐ 2

If YES was this because of:

Chest Illness (e.g. Bronchitis) ☐ 1

Accident and/or Injury ☐ 2

Tonsils/Adenoids ☐ 3

*For any other Operations_____ ☐ 4

Accidental Poisoning ☐ 5

*Please specify   *Any other Illness _____ ☐ 6

We would like to ask you some questions about the members of your household and their smoking habits, if any.

7. What is the total number of people, including this child, who live in your household?   ☐☐

8. Of that number, how many smoke cigarettes?   ☐☐

9. Does this child live with: (please tick one box only)

Both parents ☐ 1   Mother only ☐ 2

Father only ☐ 3   Foster parents ☐ 4

Others ☐ 5

10. Please tick one box in each row.
If for any row there is no such person in your household, please tick the right-hand box.

	Does not Smoke	SMOKERS Cigarettes only	SMOKERS Cigarettes & Pipe/Cigars	SMOKERS Pipe/Cigars only	Does not apply
Child's Mother or Female Guardian (YOURSELF)	☐ 1	☐ 2	☐ 3	☐ 4	☐ 5
Child's Father or Male Guardian	☐ 1	☐ 2	☐ 3	☐ 4	☐ 5
Any of the Child's Brothers	☐ 1	☐ 2	☐ 3	☐ 4	☐ 5
Any of the Child's Sisters	☐ 1	☐ 2	☐ 3	☐ 4	☐ 5
Any one of other relatives living with you	☐ 1	☐ 2	☐ 3	☐ 4	☐ 5
Anyone else in the household	☐ 1	☐ 2	☐ 3	☐ 4	☐ 5

205

11. If you used to smoke cigarettes but do not smoke them now, could you please tell me when you gave up.

This year (1978)	☐ 1	Before 1974	☐ 4
1976-1977	☐ 2	Have never smoked	☐ 5
1974-1975	☐ 3	I still smoke	☐ 6

If the child's father used to smoke cigarettes, but does not smoke now, please tell us when he gave up.

This year (1978)	☐ 1	Before 1975	☐ 4
1976-1977	☐ 2	Has never smoked	☐ 5
1974-1975	☐ 3	He still smokes	☐ 6

12. If you smoke – how many cigarettes do you smoke PER DAY? ☐

13. We would also like to ask you a few questions about your house. For each question, please place a tick against the answer which best fits your home:

Is your home	A Detached House	☐ 1
	A Semi-detached House	☐ 2
	A Terrace House	☐ 3
	A Flat or Maisonette	☐ 4
	Other	☐ 5

If otherwise please describe _____

14. Is your house mainly heated by:

Central heating? (Oil or Gas)	☐ 1	Gas fires?	☐ 4
Electric fires or Convectors (including storage heaters)	☐ 2	Paraffin stoves/heaters?	☐ 5
Open coal fires?	☐ 3	Others?	☐ 6

15. Do you use a gas water heater such as an Ascot in your kitchen?

Yes ☐ 1 No ☐ 2

16. Do you cook by:

Gas?	☐ 1	Coal?	☐ 3
Electricity?	☐ 2	Other _____	☐ 4

(please describe)

17. Could you please tell us if you and/or the child's father suffer from bronchitis?

	Yes	No
Yourself (child's mother/female guardian)	☐1	☐2
Child's father (or male guardian)	☐1	☐2

18. Here are some statements, opinions and ideas about smoking and school life. We would like you to tell us whether you agree or disagree with them. If you agree with a statement, put a tick by it in the column marked 'agree'. If you disagree, please tick the column marked 'disagree'. If you agree very much, tick the column marked 'strongly agree'. If you disagree very much tick the column marked 'strongly disagree'. If you really can't make up your mind, tick the column marked 'don't know'. Put one tick in each row.

	Strongly Agree	Agree	Don't know	Disagree	Strongly Disagree
A. Smoking does more good for a person than harm.	☐1	☐2	☐3	☐4	☐5
B. Smoking is a dirty habit.	☐1	☐2	☐3	☐4	☐5
C. I wouldn't like my children to smoke.	☐1	☐2	☐3	☐4	☐5
D. One can't tell how successful in life a person will be until they leave school.	☐1	☐2	☐3	☐4	☐5
E. There is nothing wrong with smoking	☐1	☐2	☐3	☐4	☐5
F. I am satisfied with the education my child is receiving.	☐1	☐2	☐3	☐4	☐5
G. If children and adolescents want to smoke then there's nothing adults can do about it.	☐1	☐2	☐3	☐4	☐5
H. Smoking is pleasurable.	☐1	☐2	☐3	☐4	☐5
I. Morally, no one should prevent someone else from smoking.	☐1	☐2	☐3	☐4	☐5
J. There is not enough fuss being made about the dangers of smoking.	☐1	☐2	☐3	☐4	☐5
K. Once a teenager is allowed to smoke he will probably grow up to be a heavy smoker.	☐1	☐2	☐3	☐4	☐5
L. Parents who smoke have no right to prevent their children from smoking.	☐1	☐2	☐3	☐4	☐5

207

19 Which of the following seem to you reasons for stopping or cutting down smoking?
(please tick any that apply)

        a. The expense of smoking ☐ 1

        b. The messiness or dirtiness of the habit ☐ 1

        c. Not really enjoying smoking ☐ 1

        d. The effect of smoking on my health ☐ 1

        e. Being a bad example to children and others ☐ 1

        f. Having someone want me to stop or cut down ☐ 1

        g. Other _____ ☐ 1

---

20. Were you in paid or gainful employment for more than 30 hours last week?   YES/NO

If YES please state a) your occupation _____

               b) the industry this is in _____

               c) what kind of work you do _____

_____

Are you self-employed? YES/NO

If NO Are you a Manager?   ☐ Yes   ☐ No

    Are you a Foreman?   ☐ Yes   ☐ No

---

21. Are you the head of the household? (Chief wage earner)   YES/NO
If NO please give the head of the household's exact

        a) Occupation _____

        b) Industry _____

        c) What kind of work he does _____

_____

Is the head of the household

    Self-employed?   ☐ Yes   ☐ No

    A Manager?   ☐ Yes   ☐ No

    A Foreman?   ☐ Yes   ☐ No

---

22. Please be so kind as to record your own age in years.
    Tick as appropriate

               1   2   3   4   5
    Under 34 ☐ 35-44 ☐ 45-54 ☐ 55-64 ☐ 65 and over ☐

Thank you very much for your help. This is the end of the questionnaire.

MEDICAL RESEARCH COUNCIL DERBYSHIRE STUDY

If this is not your address please write your correct address below:

....
....
....

Dear Sir/Madam,

Several weeks ago we wrote to you about the large scale study we have been carrying out in Derbyshire, in co-operation with the Area Health Authority and the Education Department. It is very important that the details requested in that letter are obtained so that we can make recommendations to the Medical Research Council about improvements in the health services. We would therefore be most grateful if you will answer the questions below.

Thank you very much for your help.
Yours faithfully,

Professor W.W. Holland.

---

1. Do you smoke cigarettes now? ....YES ☐ 1   NO ☐ 2

   If YES, how many cigarettes do you usually smoke each day?.. ☐☐

   If NO, have you ever smoked regularly

   (at least 1 cigarette a day)? ....YES ☐ 1   NO ☐ 2

---

2. What is your current occupation? .... Full-time student ... ☐ 1
   (tick one box only)   Full-time employment ☐ 2
                                                 Armed Forces .... ☐ 3
                                                 Housewife .... ☐ 4
                                                 Unemployed .... ☐ 5

   If you are in full-time employment, what kind of work do you do?

   ....

---

3. Are you married? ....YES ☐ 1   NO ☐ 2

---

4. Have you visited your doctor in the last 6 months? YES ☐ 1   NO ☐ 2

   If YES, was it for a chest complaint? ....YES ☐ 1   NO ☐ 2

---

5. Have you been admitted to hospital in the past year?
   YES ☐ 1   NO ☐ 2

Thank you.
Please return this form in the envelope provided; no stamp is required.

209

CONFIDENTIAL

If this is not your address please write
your correct address below.

_____

_____

_____

MEDICAL RESEARCH COUNCIL/DERBYSHIRE STUDY

This booklet contains a series of questions about what you have been doing since you left school. Please answer all the questions to the best of your ability. You should answer the questions by ticking the appropriate box.

YOUR REPLIES WILL BE KEPT STRICTLY CONFIDENTIAL

Thank you for your help.

This questionnaire remains the property of
Department of Community Medicine
St. Thomas's Hospital Medical School,
London SE1 7EH

210

TICK ONE BOX ONLY FOR EACH QUESTION UNLESS YOU ARE INSTRUCTED OTHERWISE

1. Are you
   - female? ☐ 1
   - male? ☐ 2

2. Are you
   - single? ☐ 1
   - married? ☐ 2
   - separated/divorced/widowed? ☐ 3
   - other? ☐ 4

3. How many children do you have? ☐

4. How old were you when you left school? ☐☐

5. Who do you live with?
   - no-one ☐ 1
   - friends ☐ 2
   - one parent ☐ 3
   - both parents ☐ 4
   - wife/husband ☐ 5
   - wife/husband and parent(s) ☐ 6
   - other ☐ 7

6. Do you own a car?
   - Yes ☐ 1
   - No ☐ 2

7. Do you own a motorbike?
   - Yes ☐ 1
   - No ☐ 2

8. Are you

   TICK ONE BOX ONLY
   - employed in full-time paid work? ☐ 1
   - employed in part-time paid work? ☐ 2
   - a full-time housewife? ☐ 3
   - a housewife with paid work outside the home? ☐ 4
   - unemployed? ☐ 5
   - a member of the armed forces? ☐ 6
   - other? ☐ 7

IF YOU HAVE NEVER WORKED GO TO QUESTION 8 PAGE 5, OTHERWISE
CONTINUE WITH THE QUESTIONS ON THE NEXT PAGE

1. PLEASE ANSWER THE FOLLOWING QUESTIONS FOR THE JOB YOU HAVE NOW.
   IF YOU ARE NOT WORKING NOW ANSWER THE QUESTIONS FOR THE LAST
   PAID JOB YOU HELD

   a. What job do you actually do? _____

   b. Did you need a particular qualification
      or training to obtain this job? _____

   c. Are you:

a manager working for an employer? ☐	1
a foreman or supervisor working for an employer? ☐	2
working for an employer? ☐	3
self-employed? ☐	4

   d. How many firms have you worked for since leaving school? ☐

2. BELOW ARE SOME ITEMS ABOUT YOUR JOB. PLEASE SHOW HOW SATISFIED
   YOU ARE WITH EACH OF THEM BY MARKING THE APPROPRIATE BOX.

	Very Dissatisfied	Quite Dissatisfied	Not Sure	Quite Satisfied	Very Satisfied
a. The amount of variety in your job	☐	☐	☐	☐	☐
b. The amount of responsibility you are given	☐	☐	☐	☐	☐
c. The freedom to choose your own method of working	☐	☐	☐	☐	☐
d. Your promotion prospects	☐	☐	☐	☐	☐
e. The attention paid to suggestions you make	☐	☐	☐	☐	☐
f. The recognition you get for good work	☐	☐	☐	☐	☐
g. The opportunities to use your abilities	☐	☐	☐	☐	☐
	(1)	(2)	(3)	(4)	(5)

3. YOU MAY HAVE FELT THAT IN THE LAST SECTION SOME OF THE THINGS
   ASKED ABOUT DID NOT APPLY TO YOUR JOB. ON THIS LIST WOULD YOU
   INDICATE HOW MUCH YOU FEEL EACH OF THESE FEATURES IS PRESENT IN
   THE JOB YOU ARE DOING NOW.

	There's none of that in my job	There's a little of that in my job	There's a moderate amount of that in my job	There's quite a lot of that in my job	There's a great deal of that in my job
a. Variety	☐	☐	☐	☐	☐
b. Responsibility	☐	☐	☐	☐	☐
c. Being able to choose your own method of working	☐	☐	☐	☐	☐
d. Chance of promotion	☐	☐	☐	☐	☐
e. Chance to use your abilities	☐	☐	☐	☐	☐
f. Recognition for good work	☐	☐	☐	☐	☐
g. Attention paid to suggestions	☐	☐	☐	☐	☐
h. Stress	☐	☐	☐	☐	☐
i. Boredom	☐	☐	☐	☐	☐
	(1)	(2)	(3)	(4)	(5)

212

4. PLEASE TICK THE APPROPRIATE BOX FOR THE FOLLOWING QUESTIONS ABOUT YOUR PRESENT JOB OR YOUR LAST PAID JOB IF YOU ARE NOT WORKING AT THE MOMENT.

		YES	NO
a.	Do you usually work alone?	☐	☐
b.	Are MOST of your workmates the same sex as yourself?	☐	☐
c.	Do you work shifts?	☐	☐
d.	Are you paid piece-rate?	☐	☐
e.	Are you required to clock-on?	☐	☐
f.	Do you work overtime regularly?	☐	☐
g.	Was this the job you wanted to do when you left school?	☐	☐
h.	Would you say you get on well with the people who have been at your workplace a lot longer than you?	☐	☐
i.	Do you have 'official' breaks which allow you to stop working for short periods of time? (apart from mealbreaks)	☐	☐
j.	Do you take breaks other than official breaks?	☐	☐
k.	Is there a special place for you to go to during breaktimes. i.e. are you able to leave your job?	☐	☐
l.	Do you usually spend your breaks talking to workmates?	☐	☐
m.	Is it possible to buy cigarettes at your place of work?	☐	☐

5. Is smoking allowed in your workplace?

	Yes, with no restrictions	☐ 1
	Yes, with limited restrictions	☐ 2
	ONLY during breaks	☐ 3
	No	☐ 4

6. Do the people you work with smoke?

	none or few of them	☐ 1
	several of them	☐ 2
	all or most of them	☐ 3

7. If your workmates smoke do they usually offer their cigarettes around?

	Yes	☐ 1
	No	☐ 2
	My workmates do not smoke	☐ 3
	I have no workmates	☐ 4

213

THESE QUESTIONS ARE FOR THOSE WITHOUT A FULL–TIME JOB OUTSIDE THE HOME.
IF YOU HAVE A JOB DO NOT ANSWER THESE QUESTIONS AND TURN OVER TO
SECTION III: LEISURE.

8. How long is it since you held a full-time job?

Less than 6 months ☐ 1

Between 6 months and 1 year ☐ 2

A year or more ☐ 3

9. How often do you do the following during the DAYTIME?

	MOST DAYS	SOME DAYS	NEVER
a. Housework	☐	☐	☐
b. Shopping	☐	☐	☐
c. Childcare	☐	☐	☐
d. Visit friends or family	☐	☐	☐
e. Nothing special	☐	☐	☐
f. Other	☐	☐	☐
	(1)	(2)	(3)

If you ticked other, please explain _____

10. Who do you USUALLY spend your time with during the day?

your husband/wife or boyfriend/girlfriend ☐ 1

one or two close friends ☐ 2

a large number of friends ☐ 3

other family members (not a husband or wife) ☐ 4

no-one ☐ 5

other ☐ 6

11. Do you plan your day in advance?

Usually ☐ 1

Sometimes ☐ 2

Never ☐ 3

214

SECTION III: LEISURE

1. How often do you do the following in the EVENING?

		MOST EVENINGS	SOME EVENINGS	NEVER
a.	Watch TV	☐	☐	☐
b.	Go to the pub	☐	☐	☐
c.	Play sport e.g. Football/Swimming	☐	☐	☐
d.	Play games e.g. Pool/Darts	☐	☐	☐
e.	Attend classes	☐	☐	☐
f.	Housework	☐	☐	☐
g.	Nothing special	☐	☐	☐
h.	Other	☐	☐	☐
		(1)	(2)	(3)

If you ticked other, please explain _____

2. How often do you do any of the following?

		DAILY	WEEKLY	MONTHLY	NEVER
a.	Go for a walk (other than going about your usual activities)	☐	☐	☐	☐
b.	Go for a run or a jog	☐	☐	☐	☐
c.	Cycle	☐	☐	☐	☐
d.	Do Keep-Fit exercises	☐	☐	☐	☐
e.	Weight training	☐	☐	☐	☐
		(1)	(2)	(3)	(4)

3. Who do you USUALLY spend your evenings with?

girlfriend/boyfriend or husband/wife	☐ 1
one or two close friends	☐ 2
large group of friends	☐ 3
family members (not a wife or husband)	☐ 4
alone	☐ 5
other	☐ 6

4. If you spend your evening with more than one other person are they usually

all female?	☐ 1
all male?	☐ 2
male and female?	☐ 3

215

5. How many of your workmates do you see socially?

      none ☐ 1

      some ☐ 2

      most ☐ 3

      I do not have workmates ☐ 4

      I do not work ☐ 5

6. Would you say that MOST of your present friends are people you grew up with?

      Yes ☐ 1

      No ☐ 2

7. Would you say that MOST of your close friends are also friends with each other?

      Yes ☐ 1

      No ☐ 2

8. When in the pub do you play darts or pool or other pub games?

      Always ☐ 1

      Sometimes ☐ 2

      Never ☐ 3

      I do not go to the pub ☐ 4

9. How much alcohol do you usually drink each week?

      Wine ☐ ☐ glasses

      Lager/Beer ☐ ☐ pints

      Cider ☐ ☐ pints

      Spirits ☐ ☐ single measures

10. How much alcohol do you drink?

      A little ☐ 1

      A moderate amount ☐ 2

      Quite a lot ☐ 3

      A lot ☐ 4

      I do not drink alcohol ☐ 5

11. How many of the friends you usually spend time with outside work smoke?

      None or a few of them ☐ 1

      Several of them ☐ 2

      Most or all of them ☐ 3

12. If your friends smoke do they usually offer their cigarettes around?

      Yes ☐ 1

      No ☐ 2

      My friends do not smoke ☐ 3

1. Have you EVER smoked?   Yes ☐ 1

    If you answered NO, go to question 19   No   ☐ 2

---

2. Do you smoke now? (Tick one box only)   Daily   ☐ 1

                                                     Occasionally ☐ 2

                                                     Not at all   ☐ 3

    If you answered NOT AT ALL go to question 18, otherwise continue to answer the following
    questions.

---

3. What do you USUALLY smoke?

                                         manufactured cigarettes ☐ 1

                                         hand rolled cigarettes ☐ 2

                                                           pipe ☐ 3

                                                         cigars ☐ 4

---

4. What brand of cigarettes/cigars do you usually smoke or what kind of tobacco?
    Please give brand name and tar level.

    Brand name: _____

    Tar Level: _____

---

5. a. If you smoke cigarettes, how many do you smoke a day on weekdays?   ☐☐

       How many cigarettes a day do you usually smoke at weekends?   ☐☐

       b. If you smoke a pipe or roll your own cigarettes, how many ounces or grams   ☐☐ ounces
       of tobacco do you usually smoke each week?   ☐☐ grams

       c. If you smoke cigars, how many cigars a week do you usually smoke?   ☐☐

---

6. PEOPLE SMOKE DIFFERENT AMOUNTS IN DIFFERENT PLACES. PLEASE INDICATE
    HOW MANY CIGARETTES YOU SMOKE OR WHETHER YOU SMOKE A PIPE OR
    CIGARS IN THE FOLLOWING SITUATIONS.

    Cigarettes (including hand-rolled)

	NONE	1–5	6–10	11–15	16/over	Pipe/Cigars
a. At work or at home DURING THE DAY	☐	☐	☐	☐	☐	☐
b. At home IN THE EVENING	☐	☐	☐	☐	☐	☐
c. Out socially IN THE EVENING	☐	☐	☐	☐	☐	☐
	(1)	(2)	(3)	(4)	(5)	(6)

217

7. How often do you share your cigarettes with the following?

		USUALLY	SOMETIMES	NEVER
a.	Family	☐	☐	☐
b.	Workmates	☐	☐	☐
c.	Friends	☐	☐	☐
		(1)	(2)	(3)

8. How often do you smoke ALONE in the following situations?

		USUALLY	SOMETIMES	NEVER
a.	At home	☐	☐	☐
b.	At work	☐	☐	☐
c.	Socially	☐	☐	☐
		(1)	(2)	(3)

9. Do you inhale tobacco smoke?

Yes ☐ 1
Sometimes ☐ 2
No ☐ 3

10. How old were you when you started to smoke regularly? ☐☐ years

11a. Have you ever tried to give up smoking altogether?

Never ☐ 1
Once ☐ 2
Two or three times ☐ 3
More than three times ☐ 4

11b. How many times have you given up smoking for a week or more? ☐☐

12. Would you like to give up smoking?

Yes ☐ 1
I do not care ☐ 2
No ☐ 3

If you answered YES, what is the MAIN reason?

cost ☐ 1
concern for your health ☐ 2
pregnancy ☐ 3
doctor's advice ☐ 4
something you read or saw on TV ☐ 5
pressure from friends or family ☐ 6
other ☐ 7

If you answered other, please give details _____

218

| 13. | Do you think you would feel healthier if you gave up smoking? | Yes | ☐ | 1 |
| | | No | ☐ | 2 |

| 14. | Are you concerned about putting on weight if you gave up smoking? | Yes | ☐ | 1 |
| | | No | ☐ | 2 |

15.	How difficult do you think it would be for you to give up smoking?	Very difficult	☐	1
		Quite difficult	☐	2
		Not at all difficult	☐	3

16.	Do you ever limit your smoking because of pressure from family or friends?	Always	☐	1
		Sometimes	☐	2
		Never	☐	3

17. TO HELP US UNDERSTAND WHY PEOPLE SMOKE MORE IN CERTAIN SITUATIONS, PLEASE SHOW WHETHER YOU AGREE OR DISAGREE WITH THE FOLLOWING STATEMENTS BY TICKING THE CORRECT BOX. PLEASE ANSWER FOR EACH SITUATION, AT WORK, AT HOME AND SOCIALLY.

| | | AT WORK | | AT HOME | | SOCIALLY | |
		Agree	Disagree	Agree	Disagree	Agree	Disagree
a.	I smoke to keep myself from slowing down	☐	☐	☐	☐	☐	☐
b.	Handling and lighting up a cigarette is part of the enjoyment of smoking it	☐	☐	☐	☐	☐	☐
c.	Smoking is pleasant and relaxing	☐	☐	☐	☐	☐	☐
d.	When I feel uncomfortable, upset or angry about something, I smoke	☐	☐	☐	☐	☐	☐
e.	I smoke when I am bored	☐	☐	☐	☐	☐	☐
f.	I really want to smoke if I haven't done so for a while	☐	☐	☐	☐	☐	☐
g.	I smoke automatically without being aware of it	☐	☐	☐	☐	☐	☐
h.	I smoke when I have nothing to do	☐	☐	☐	☐	☐	☐
		(1)	(2)	(1)	(2)	(1)	(2)

● ● ● ● ● GO TO QUESTION 19 ● ● ● ● ●

219

18a. How often did you smoke?

Daily ☐ 1

Occasionally ☐ 2

Only once or twice ☐ 3

18b. How long is it since you gave up smoking?

Less than a week ☐ 1

One week to one month ☐ 2

More than one month but less than a year ☐ 3

More than a year ☐ 4

18c. What was it like for you to give up smoking?

Very hard ☐ 1

Quite hard ☐ 2

Not hard at all ☐ 3

18d. What was the MAIN reason for you giving up?

cost ☐ 1

concern for your health ☐ 2

doctor's advice ☐ 3

pregnancy ☐ 4

something you read or saw on TV ☐ 5

pressure from friends or family ☐ 6

other ☐ 7

If other, please explain _____

19. What do you think you will be doing in 10 years time?

smoking 20 cigarettes or more a day	1
smoking less than 20 cigarettes a day	2
smoking cigarettes only occasionally	3
smoking a pipe or cigars	4
not smoking at all	5

20. Please describe the smoking habits of each person listed below. Tick one box in each row.

		Does not Smoke	Smokes Cigarettes Occasionally	Smokes Cigarettes Regularly	Smokes Pipe/Cigars ONLY	Does Not Apply
a.	Wife/husband Boyfriend/girlfriend					
b.	Mother					
c.	Father					
		(1)	(2)	(3)	(4)	(5)

21. How many people of your age smoke?

hardly any	1
some	2
quite a lot	3
most	4

22. HERE ARE SOME OPINIONS AND IDEAS ABOUT SMOKING. PLEASE INDICATE HOW MUCH YOU AGREE WITH THE STATEMENTS BY TICKING THE APPROPRIATE BOX.

		Strongly Agree	Agree	Don't Know	Disagree	Strongly Disagree
a.	Smoking is only bad for you if you have been smoking for many years					
b.	Smoking is dangerous only to older people					
c.	Smoking is only bad for you if you smoke a lot					
		(1)	(2)	(3)	(4)	(5)

221

SECTION V: TIME

13. TO HELP US UNDERSTAND MORE ABOUT HOW PEOPLE MANAGE THEIR TIME, PLEASE ANSWER THE FOLLOWING QUESTIONS FOR WHEN YOU ARE AT WORK, AT HOME AND OUT SOCIALLY. PLEASE ANSWER FOR EACH SITUATION.

		AT WORK		AT HOME		OUT SOCIALLY	
		yes	no	yes	no	yes	no
a.	Do you usually know what time it is without looking at your watch?	☐	☐	☐	☐	☐	☐
b.	Do you usually care what time it is?	☐	☐	☐	☐	☐	☐
c.	Do you often feel that time drags by?	☐	☐	☐	☐	☐	☐
d.	Do you feel you often waste your time?	☐	☐	☐	☐	☐	☐
e.	Are you often surprised at how quickly time has passed?	☐	☐	☐	☐	☐	☐
		(1)	(2)	(1)	(2)	(1)	(2)

SECTION VI: HEALTH

HEALTH

1. People think of health in different ways. Which of the following do you think BEST describes health? (Tick one box only)

   Ability to carry on with usual activities ☐ 1
   Fitness ☐ 2
   State of body ☐ 3
   State of mind ☐ 4

2. How would you describe your health over the past 12 months?

   excellent ☐ 1
   good ☐ 2
   fair ☐ 3
   poor ☐ 4

3. Do you ever do things to keep healthy?

   never ☐ 1
   occasionally ☐ 2
   regularly ☐ 3

   If you do things to keep healthy, what are they? _____

_____

222

4. During the last six months have you done any of the following?

		YES	NO
a.	Visited your doctor for anything other than contraceptive reasons	☐	☐
b.	Been so ill you have had to stay in bed	☐	☐
c.	Taken any medication	☐	☐
d.	Been to hospital out-patients for any reason, eg. x-ray, ante-natal care	☐	☐
e.	Been admitted to hospital	☐	☐
		(1)	(2)

If you have been admitted to hospital,
what was this for? _____

---

5. BELOW IS A LIST OF THINGS SOME PEOPLE DO. PLEASE TICK THE BOXES
AS THEY APPLY TO YOU.

		YES	NO
a.	Do you usually weigh yourself at least once a week?	☐	☐
b.	Do you usually use margarine instead of butter?	☐	☐
c.	Do you usually drink skimmed milk?	☐	☐
d.	Do you usually brush your teeth daily?	☐	☐
e.	Do you usually eat wholemeal bread?	☐	☐
f.	Do you usually take sugar in tea or coffee?	☐	☐
		(1)	(2)

		YES	NO
i.	Do you usually cough first thing in the morning in winter?	☐	☐
ii.	Do you usually bring up any phlegm from your chest first thing in the morning in winter?	☐	☐
iii.	Do you bring up any phlegm from your chest during the day in winter?	☐	☐
iv.	If you answered YES to questions ii or iii, do you bring up phlegm like this for as much as three months each year?	☐	☐
v.	Do you get short of breath when hurrying on flat ground or walking up a slight hill?	☐	☐
		(1)	(2)

Thank you very much for completing this questionnaire. Please check to see that you have answered all the questions. If you have any other comments which you think will be helpful, please write them below.

After you have completed the questionnaire, please return it in the envelope provided.

Appendix II: Definition of variables

ACD - **Unorganised social activities:**
'Mess around','Go around with a group the same age'
1. Does neither.
2. Does at least one of these.

ACO - **Organised social activities:**
Goes to the cinema, dancingor to a youth club
1. Does none of these.
2. Does at least one of these.

ACS - **Social activities:**
1. No more than one of five socialactivities
2. Two or more of the five

ASC - **Anti-school attitudes:**
'I am fed up with school'
'It is alright to tell a lie to a teacher to get out of trouble'
1.Did not strongly agree or agree to either.
2. Strongly agreed or agreed to one of these.

ASM - **Anti-smoking attitudes:**
'Cigarettes should be harder toget'
'Smoking is a dirty habit'
'Children caught smokingshould be punished'
1. Did not strongly agree or agree to any ofthese.
2. Strongly agreed or agreed to at least one of these.

COM - **Companionship:**
With whom do you spend MOST of your time?
1. Alone or with parents
2. Same sex friends
3. Oppositesex friends

EMPS - **Employment status in 1984:**
1. Full-time work.
2.Part-time work.
3. Full-time housewife.
4. Housewife and paid work.
5. Unemployed.
6. Armed forces.
7. Other (mainly students).

FSM - **Favourable attitudes to smoking:**
'Smoking can help people when they feel nervous or embarrassed'
Smoking is very enjoyable'
'There is nothing wrong with smoking'
1. Did not strongly agree or agree to any of these.
2. Strongly agreed or agreed to at least one of these.

HAZ - **Awareness of hazards of smoking:**
Three attitude statements implied that hazards only apply to the
old, to the long term or to the heavy smokers.
1. Did not agree to any of the three
2. Agreed to one or more of the three

INJS - **Intrinsic job satisfaction:**
Seven job characteristics -
variety;
responsibility;
choice of work; promotion prospects;
responsiveness to suggestions;
recognition of work;
chance to use abilities.
1. Not satisfied with more than 3 of these.
2. Satisfied with 4 or more of these.

PCN - **Parental concern about smoking:**
'My parents are stricter than my teachers about smoking'
'My parents don't allow me to smoke'
    1. Did not strongly agree or agree to either.
    2. Strongly agreed or agreed to one of these.

PER - **Peer pressure:**
Three attitude statements indicated susceptibility to peer pressure to smoke
    1. Did not agree two any of three
    2. Agreed with at least one of the three

PPM - **Parental permissiveness:**
'My parents do not mind whom I go around with'
'My parents are upset if I do badly in my schoolwork'
'My parents would like me to get a better job than my father's when I leave school'
    1. Disagreed with the first and agreed with the other two.
    2. Either agreed with the first or disagreed with one of the others.

PSM - **Parental smoking in 1974**
    1. Neither
    2. Mother
    3. Father
    4. Both

PS78 - **Parental smoking in 1978**
    1. Neither
    2. Mother
    3. Father
    4.Both

PS84 - **Parental smoking in 1984**
    1. Neither
    2. Mother
    3. Father
    4.Both

SBS - **Sibling smoking**
    1 No siblings
    2. Non-smoking siblings
    3. Smoking siblings

SC74 - **Social class of the parents in 1974**
    1. For I, II and IIInm
    2 for IIm, IV and V
    3 for unknowm

SC84   -   **Social class of the young adults in 1984**
          1. For I, II and IIInm
          2 for IIm, IV and V
          3 for unknowm (unemployed, students etc.)

SEX   -   1 for males and
          2 for females

SHFT   -   **Shiftwork in 1984**
          1. No.
          2. Yes. SPG

        -   **Plays sports or games - 1974**
          1. No.
          2. Yes.

SPOR   -   **Plays sport in the evening 1984**
          1. No.
          2. Yes.

SPSM   -   **Spouses smoking:**
          1. Non-smoker.
          2. Occasional smoker.
          3. Regular smoker.
          4. Pipe or cigars.
          5. Not applicable.

S74A   -   **Child's smoking in 1974 (4 categories)**
          1. Never smoked.
          2. Tried once.
          3. Occasional.
          4. One or more a week.

S78   -   **Child's smoking in 1978**
          1. Never smoked.
          2. Tried once.
          3. Occasional.
          4. 1-6 cigarettes a week.
          5. More than 6 cigarettes a week.
          6. Ex-smoker.

S84   -   1. Daily
          2. Occasionally
          3. Ex-smoker
          4. Non-smoker (never really smoked)

Appendix III: Study publications

1. Bland, J.M., Bewlwy, B.R., Banks, H.M., Pollard, V. (1975) Schoolchildren's beliefs about smoking and disease. Health Education Journal, 34 (3): **71-78**
2. Banks, M.H., Bewley, B.R., Bland, J.M., Dean, J.R., Pollard, V. (1978) Long-term study of smoking by secondary schoolchildren Archives of Disease in Childhood, 53 (1): **12-19**
3. Bewley, B.R. (1978) Smoking in childhood. Postgraduate Medical Journal, 54: **197-198**
4. Bland, J.M., Bewley, B.R., Pollard, B., Banks, M.H. (1978) Effect of children's and parents' smoking on respiratory symptoms. Archives of Disease in Childhood. 53 (2): **100-105**
5. Bewley, B.R., Johnson, M.R.D., Banks, M.H (1979). Teachers' smoking. Journal of Epidemiology and Community Health, 33 (3): **219-222**
6. Bland, J.M., Bewley, B.R., Banks, M.H. (1979) Cigarette smoking and children's respiratory symptoms: Validity of the questionnaire method. Revue Epidemiologie et Sante Publique, **27:69-76**
7. Bewley, B.R., Johnson, M.R.D., Bland, J.M., Murray, M. (1980) Trends in children's smoking. Community Medicine, 2: **180-189**

229

8. Murray, M., Cracknell, A. (1980) Adolescents' views of smoking
   Journal of Psychosomatic Research, 24: *243-251*

9. Banks, M.H., Bewley, B.R., Bland, J.M. (1981). Adolescent attitudes to smoking: their influence on behaviour.
   International Journal of Health Education, 24 (1): **39-44**

10. Johnson, M.R.D., Murray, M., Bewley, B.R., Clyde, D.C., Banks, M.H., Swan, A.V. (1982). Social Class, parents, children and smoking
    Bulletin of the International Union against Tuberculosis 57,
    (3-4): **258-262**

11. Murray, M. Swan, A.V., Johnson, M.R.D., Bewley, B.R. (1983) Some factors associated with increased risk of smoking by children.
    Journal of Child Psychology and Psychiatry, 24 (2): **223-232**

12. Murray, M., Swan, A.V., Bewley, B.R., Johnson, M.R.D. (1983). The development of smoking during adolescence - The MRC/Derbyshire Smoking Study. International Journal of Epidemiology, 12 (2): **185-192**

13. Murray, M., Kiryluk, S., Swan, A.V. (1984). School characteristics and adolescent smoking. J. Epidemiology and Community Health,
    38: **167-172**

14. Murray, M., Jarrett, L., (1985). Young peoples' perception of health, illness and smoking.
    Health Education Journal, 44 (1): **18-22**

15. Murray, M., Jarrett, L., (1985). Young peoples' perception of smoking at work. Health Education Journal, 44 (1): **22-26**

16. Murray, M., Kiryluk, S., Swan, A.V. (1985). Relation between parents' and children's smoking behaviour and attitudes. J. Epidemiology and Community Health, 39: **169-174**

17. Johnson, M.R.D., Bewley, B.R., Banks, M.H., Bland, J.M., Clyde, D.V., smoking at school. British J. Educational Psychology 55, **34-44**

18. Murray, M., (1983). The social context of smoking during adolescence
    In Forbes WF (Ed) Proceedings of Fifth World
    Conference on Smoking and Health

19. Bewley, B.R., Bland, JM., Murray, M., Swan, A.V. (In Press) Cigarette smoking and the development of respiratory symptoms in adolescents.
    Preventive Medicine

20. Murray, M., Swan A.V., Kiryluk S. and Clarke G.C. (1988) The Hawthorne effect in the measurement of adolescent smoking.
    J Epid and Comm Health 42, No.3, **p304-306**

21. Swan A.V., Creeser R., Murray M. (1990) Whan and why children first start to smoke. Int J Epidemiol 12: **323-30.**

230

Other papers on smoking

1. Murray, M., Swan, A.V., Mattar, N. (1981). Smoking among new student nurses. Journal of Advanced Nursing, 6: **255-260.**
2. Murray, M., Swan, A.V., Mattar, N. (1983) The task of nursing and the risk of smoking. Journal of Advanced Nursing, 8: **131-138**
3. Murray, M., Swan, A.V., Johnson, M.R.D., Enock, G., Reid, D., Banks, M.H.(1982). The effectiveness of the 'My Body' school health education project. Health Education Journal, 41: **126-130**
4. Murray, M., Rona, R., Morris, R., Tait, N. (1984) The smoking and dietary practices of Lambeth schoolchildren I: The effectiveness of an anti-smoking and nutrition education
programme for children. Public Health (London), 98: **163-172**
5. Murray, M., Swan, A.V., Clarke, G . (1984). Long-term effect of a school-based anti-smoking programme. J. Epidemiology and Community Health, 38: **247-252**
6. Morris, M., Rona, R., Murray, M., Green, V., Shah, D. (2984) The smoking and dietary practices of Lambeth schoolchildren II: The relationship between knowledge, attitudes and behaviour. Public Health (London), 98: **225-232**
7. Withey C.H., Price C.E., Swan A.V., Papacosta A.O., Hensley M.J. (1988) Repeatability of a Questionnaire to assess respiratory symptoms in smokers. J Epidemiol and Community Health 42, No.1, **p54-59**
8. Young D., Swan A.V., Melia J. (1989) Cigarette Advertising and the Youth Market Health Educ J 48, 3, **p113-116**